# How NOT To Use Your Smartphone (or Tablet)

Rodney D. Cambridge

**How NOT To Use Your Smartphone (or Tablet)**

Copyright 2012, Rodney D. Cambridge

Published by Rodney D. Cambridge

Also by Rod Cambridge:

**How NOT To Write an App** on **www.HowNotToBooks.co.uk**

Rodney D. Cambridge

In memory of Aunty Una.

# Table of Contents

# Preface

Picture the scene: Its Summer 2012 and you've just touched down in London, tickets primed, to watch your favourite events at the Olympic Games. You check into the Days Suite hotel, kick off your shoes, and sink back into a comfortable chair after a long and tiring journey.

You've been out of the loop for the last 12 hours so you take out your smartphone to see if you're able to pick up email. Luckily your phone picks up the Days Suite Wi-Fi network and within seconds you're online without even having to enter a password. Result! Why can't *all* hotels be so accommodating?

Every evening for the next week, after spending your days taking in the London landmarks and watching the Games, you use the free Days Suite Wi-Fi to keep in touch with your friends and family, update your social networks, check your bank balances, and conduct other financial transactions.

When it's time to check out, you settle up with the receptionist and thank him for the use of the free Wi-Fi.

But he looks at you blankly and informs you that Days Suite doesn't have free Wi-Fi.

Confused, you shrug your shoulders, jump into the waiting taxi, and head for the airport. You have a long journey ahead.

**But what just happened?**

Unfortunately for you, the Days Suite Wi-Fi network was not what it seemed. And you've just become a victim of identity theft.

You see, some really clever people (who we'll call 'the bad guys') decided to set up a fake Wi-Fi network near to your hotel with the sole intention of getting hold of your money and personal information. Rather sneakily, they called it the *Days Suite* network in order to trick you into thinking it was a service provided by the hotel. All they had to do was sit back and wait for someone to log on. Remember, the bad guys are *really* clever.

**But what does this mean?**

Well, every time you used their network to log into FaceBook or Twitter to update your status, or Flickr to post your pictures, or into your email or your bank account, the bad guys were 'eavesdropping'. Because it's their network they were able to see everything going through it. This means that they were able to see, and make copies of, your credentials including your account names and passwords, or any other confidential information that you might have typed in such as your date of birth or your mother's maiden name. When they have enough of your information, they can then log into those online services as you. They can then do all the things that you would normally do such as transfer funds from one account to another, read and respond to email, or post status updates to your social networks.

This type of attack is known as a man in the middle attack because, well, the bad guy inserts himself in the middle – right between your device and the internet. And by doing so, he ensures that all information being sent to and from your device goes via him and his computer systems where he can make copies of it.

Remember that long journey you have ahead? Well, it's going to get even longer. Because once your information has been taken in this way, it may take months before any fraudulent activity becomes apparent. And during this time, your credit rating will, no doubt, be adversely affected. In addition, it can take months, or even years, before everything finally gets put right.

In this scenario, prevention is most definitely better than cure.

**How it all could have been avoided**

There's a very simple way that getting caught out by the bad guys could have been avoided:

*Whenever you check into a hotel, ask if they have Wi-Fi.*

If they do, they will probably hand you a leaflet then and there detailing the name of the Wi-Fi network and the passcode in order to access it. If they don't have a leaflet, ask them to write the details down for you.

This way, you'll know that the Wi-Fi network that you connect to is the hotel's legitimate network and not something thrown up by someone hoping to trick you into logging in so that they can make some money out of you.

For the last 18 years, I've worked in the computer security industry. I've been busting computer viruses and other cyber threats for longer than I can remember - and not much surprises me anymore. However, seeing a supposedly tech-savvy relative of mine get stung by hackers using the method described above really *did* surprise me. He managed to get duped via a method similar to this while on a business trip to New York. By the time he realised, a string of applications for credit cards and loans had been made in his name.

This made me realise that while these smartphones are becoming more and more powerful, they're also becoming more and more dangerous and increasingly difficult to manage for the average user. And with this realisation comes a real need to explain to people where they're going wrong (through no fault of their own) when setting up and using their smartphones and tablets, and how they can make their devices work for them instead of against them.

That's why I wrote this eBook.

\*\*\*

## A Tai Chi fable

A Tai Chi master came to the village to catch a tiger. Upon finding the tiger, the master looked into its eyes. Without any struggle, the tiger fell to its knees. The master sat on the tiger's back and rode it to the mountain. While sitting on the back of the tiger, the master attained enlightenment.

Thereafter, the master returned from the mountain to help enlighten others.

# Intended Audience

This book is intended for anyone who owns a smartphone or tablet, or intends on purchasing one soon, who is unsure about the security risks that come with owning and using these powerful devices. If you're already knowledgeable about security threats, this book may not be for you.

If you've just bought a smartphone for your partner, teenage son or daughter, or even your parents, this book will advise them how to use it sensibly, safely, and securely, minimising the potential of their new device being used to gain access to their, and by proxy your, personal data and information.

Owning one of these devices can be a fantastic experience, but it can also be fraught with danger. However, by following the advice in this book, you'll see that it doesn't have to be.

This book is divided into lessons. While each lesson can be taken and read as a standalone unit, it makes sense to read them in the logical order in which they're presented. In addition some lessons build on, and refer to, previous lessons.

If you've been unlucky enough to have been made a victim of identity theft, fraud, hacking, etc. you need to do something about it as soon as possible. In any of these scenarios, time is of the essence so go straight to the first lesson in this book: *First Things First*. In this first section you'll find practical advice and contact information that you'll find handy.

In order to keep things easy to understand, I've tried to keep the techno-speak to a minimum in this book. However, I've also included a Glossary at the back for any terms that you don't fully understand.

So if you're ready, let's get started.

# Lesson 1: First things first

If you are ever made a victim of phone hacking, identity theft, or related crimes, you'll want to know what to steps to take. And fast.

Identity thieves don't hang about. Once you've been hacked, they'll waste no time in either using your information to attempt to obtain goods and services at your expense, or they'll sell your details on to a third party. In many cases, they'll do both - so time is of the essence.

Even if you think that only your email has been compromised, you need to change passwords to all of your online accounts and even think about closing some. Someone else having access to your email is definitely not a good thing - it means that online accounts can easily be opened on various websites in your name and verified via your email account. And just so that you don't realise, the bad guys will log in to your email and delete any emails they don't want you to see. So having access to your email password means they have access to a whole lot more.

Identity thieves can do an awful lot of bad once they have your personal information. Here are just a few of the things you may have to deal with if you are a victim:

- Financial and banking fraud
- Credit card fraud
- Governmental fraud
- Phone or utilities fraud
- Loss of social reputation
- Loss of professional reputation

For example, if the bad guys get access to your phone they can cause it make calls to premium numbers that they have set up and own, resulting in you getting massive phone bills at the end of your bill cycle. And don't think they need physical access to your phone in order to do this; in most cases, the phone will still be in your possession while the bad guys control it remotely. In addition, some types of hacks result in SMS (text) messages being sent to premium numbers every few minutes, eating up your credit if you are on Pay As You Go or, again, resulting in large bills if you are contract.

Of course when they have your details, the bad guys can even apply for and obtain a new phone and contract in your name. To make sure that you don't suspect, they'll try to change the billing address from your real address to something else, or opt out of paper bills all together. This way, you never even get to see the bills until it's way too late.

The bad guys can also apply for and attempt to open credit card accounts in your name. If successful, they'll attempt to max them out as quickly as possible – obviously with no intention of ever paying the bill. Because, again, it'll be in your name.

As before, they use the same tricks of changing the billing address immediately, or switching to paperless billing in order to cover their tracks. Because of this, it'll be months before you realise that something's up. When the accounts don't get paid, the defaults will appear on your credit record, wrecking your financial reputation.

In a similar way, the bad guys may attempt to open bank accounts in your name or obtain bank loans. If they're successful in opening a bank account, they can then issue cheques in your name - making purchases that, again, will take some time to show up on your account.

It's not only limited to phone and banking fraud, though; identity thieves can also use your details to apply for utility services such as cable TV or broadband internet services. Some have even been known to use your details to pay for their gas and electricity!

Identity thieves don't always use your information themselves. They will frequently sell your information to other unscrupulous individuals and gangs who will then attempt to forge passports, with your details, or even create and sell fake driving licences containing your name but someone else's picture.

If your National Insurance number/Social Security number are also compromised and end up in the clutches of the identity thieves, they may also attempt to apply for jobs in your name, rent houses in your name, obtain medical services, or other governmental or social benefits.

Of course, there are many other things that the bad guys will attempt to do in your name, but the examples above should make it easy to see that identity theft is a bad thing; you could end up seriously out of pocket, being arrested, and even be taken to court.

And all of these things can come about through the misuse or misconfiguration of your smartphone or tablet, in addition to you not taking sensible measures when accessing online services through your device.

You may already be a victim of identity theft if any of the following has occurred:

- Items have appeared on your bank or credit card statements that you have not purchased.

- Your application for state/social benefits has been denied as you have been told that you are already claiming.

- You have been refused loans or credit cards after previously having a good credit history.

- You have received bills or invoices for goods or services that you haven't ordered.

- You have received letters regarding debts that are not yours.

**What if it's too late?**

The aim of this book is to reduce the likelihood of you being hacked through your smartphone or tablet and ending up with the problems described above. However, unfortunately, some of us do become victims - and when that happens action must be taken quickly to minimise the reputational and financial damage that might occur.

If you believe you have been a victim, use the following information to alert the relevant organisations and authorities.

**NOTE:** For brevity, I have only listed the USA and UK contact details. If you reside in a different country, the websites below contain links and details for contacts in your country.

**What you need to do**

Place a fraud alert on your credit report. This can stop the bad guys from opening more accounts in your name. When they attempt to do so and the relevant company runs a credit check before opening the account, the fraud alert will be seen. This is an effective method of minimising the damage an identity thief can do.

You can place a fraud report on your file, or report the fact that you have become a victim, by contacting either one of the following:

**Equifax:**
USA: www.equifax.com, 1-800-525-6285, P.O. Box 740241, Atlanta, GA

30374-0241
UK: www.equifax.co.uk, 0870 010 0583, P.O. Box 1140, Bradford, BD1 5US

**Experian:**
USA: www.experian.com, 1-888-EXPERIAN (397-3742). P.O. Box 9554, Allen, TX 75013
UK: www.experian.co.uk, 0870 241 6212, P.O. Box 9000, Nottingham, NG80 7WP

**TransUnion** (USA): www.transunion.com, 1-800-680-7289. Fraud Division, P.O. Box 6790, Fullerton, CA 92834-6790

**Callcredit** (UK): www.callcredit.plc.uk, 0870 060 1414, P.O. Box 491, Leeds, LS3 1WZ

## Credit reports

Obtain a copy of your credit report. After filing a fraud alert as described above, request that the companies send you a copy of your credit report. When you get this, review it carefully to see if you can spot any anomalies. For example, you might see a string of enquires from credit card companies when you know you haven't applied for a credit card recently. This shows that someone has been attempting to obtain a credit card, loan, or some other financial service in your name. If you're in the US you can get a free credit check every year – go to www.annualcreditreport.com for more details. Depending on the country you're in you may also be able to a credit report for a minimal charge.

Change *all* of your passwords. It's no good just changing one; all of your passwords to *all* of your accounts and online services (FaceBook, Twitter, eBay, Amazon, etc.) should be changed immediately since you may not be sure which accounts have been compromised. If the identity thief still has access to one of your accounts, before you know it, he'll have access to more.

Consider closing accounts that you know have definitely been hacked. Work with the financial institution, phone company, utility company, etc. to close down any compromised account and open new ones. In addition, insist that any fraudulently opened accounts in your name are closed.

Notify your banks, credit card companies and other financial institutions in writing. Also it's important that letters to and from you are kept and copied. Your letters should include all details known to you, including relevant dates and times.

## Be proactive

Lastly, if you suspect you may become a victim of identity theft, consider registering with a service like CIFAS (www.cifas.org.uk), where a protective registration can be made by individuals against their own address when they have good reason to believe it may be used by identity thieves - for example, when a passport or drivers licence has been lost or stolen.

# Lesson 2: Traveling tips

Before we jump into the nitty-gritty of how not to use your smartphone (or tablet), it's probably a good idea to cover some travel-related do's and don'ts as I'm guessing that a fair amount of you will soon be about to embark on a vacation or trip somewhere, or are even reading this book while already sitting on a coach, train, or plane.

When getting ready to travel, your smartphone is generally the last thing you think about. I mean, it's just a smartphone – so as long as you have the charger packed you're all set, right?

Well, not quite. Just a little preparation before you jet off can save you an awful lot of hassle down the line, and so it's worth bearing some of these tips in mind before you hit the road:

**Ensure that you have enabled a PIN or password.** This is a no-brainer. Make sure that some type of security code has to be entered in order to gain access to your device. This is your first line of defence if someone gets hold of your smartphone or tablet but one that many people don't bother to implement.

**Make the PIN/Password kick in sooner.** Most smartphones enable you to increase or decrease the period of inactivity before a passcode is required to gain access. If you're traveling, change your settings so that the passcode is required every time you wake the device from sleep. It might be mildly inconvenient to keep entering your passcode, but it's certainly more secure. And when your trip is over, you can reset it back to the way you prefer.

**Make sure you Sync (or back up) your smartphone or tablet** before you leave. Even though your device is expensive, in many cases the information stored on the device is even more expensive. If your device is lost, having a full back up on your computer at home can be a life-saver. It also means that if your device is recovered, or you get a replacement, you can restore your data to the device just how it was before you left.

**Make sure your Operating System software is up to date.** Gone are the days when you'd buy a phone and expect to stay on the same system software forever. Nowadays, smartphones and tablets get system updates on a regular basis. These updates frequently contain fixes to exploits and other security holes, so it's important to be on the latest version before you travel. This goes for new devices, too; many new devices sometimes sit in their boxes for months on end, meaning that they miss out on new system updates, so make sure that you check the manufacturer's website and update your device if necessary.

**Turn on features that will enable you to track your phone.** In the unfortunate event that your device gets mislaid, you want to make it as easy as possible to recover it. For example, if you have an iOS device, turn on the *Find my iPhone* feature. These types of features will allow you to track the device to within metres. **IMPORTANT**: If you suspect someone has taken your device, do not try to retrieve it yourself if you locate it. Instead, inform local law enforcement and rely on them to retrieve the device for you.

**Enable the Remote Lock and/or Wipe features.** Not all devices have these features, but if yours does make sure that you enable it and understand how to use it. If you believe a criminal has your device in their possession, remote wipe it immediately; better that they only have your phone, and not your phone and your personal data as well. If you are lucky enough to recover your phone, you'll be able to restore the backup you took before you set off on your vacation.

**Don't connect to Wi-Fi hotspots that do not have a password.** If a hotspot doesn't have a password, it's insecure. And you shouldn't log into insecure Wi-Fi hotspots. See *Lesson 6* for more information about Wi-Fi hotspots.

**Turn off Auto-fill on your browser.** Auto-fill is a feature that many browsers have where your usernames and passwords are automatically filled-in when you visit websites that need a login. Turning this feature off means that if you do need to use a Wi-Fi network, your login credentials will not be sent over the Wi-Fi automatically; you'll be able to decide when and where your details are sent.

**Check to see if your travel insurance covers your smartphone or tablet.** If not, consider upgrading your current cover if available. Remember that as well as covering your smartphone, many of these schemes also cover cameras, iPods and other gadgets. As always, read the small print to fully understand what is and isn't covered.

**Don't conduct financial transactions over a Wi-Fi hotspot.** It's safer to wait and do this from home. If you need to check to see how much money you have in your account, visit an ATM machine or look for a local branch of your bank. If you know you have bills to pay that will come due while you're traveling, why not set them up to be paid on a particular day? Most online banking systems now allow you to automate the payment of bills on specified days of the month.

**Never use your debit card online**. If you absolutely, definitely, positively need to make a purchase online while you're traveling and you have to choose between your credit or debit cards, **never** use your debit card. This is because of the very important difference between credit cards and debit cards; with credit cards you can decline to pay any fraudulent charges that appear on the card simply by calling the credit card company and telling them that you did not make the purchase. They'll then stop the charge and enter into a dispute with the seller on your behalf. This way, your current/checking account isn't impacted and you won't be out of pocket. However purchases made on your debit card are drawn straight from your current/checking account immediately. You'll still need to call your bank in order to get things fixed, but in the meantime the money has already been taken from your account, and it might take some time before the bank decides to refund that money back to you. Typically that can take weeks but in extreme cases can take months.

## Let's get physical.

It's not all about digital security, though. When traveling with expensive gadgets and equipment you also need to ensure that you take care of physical security. Thieves are always on the lookout for easy targets, so bear the following tips in mind:

## Keep a low profile

When thieves are on the lookout for something to steal, that shiny new tablet is a prime target. Be as discreet as possible when using your device and try to keep its usage to a minimum in busy places. By having it constantly on show, you're effectively saying *"Hey – look at me! I have a mega-expensive gadget here!"*

Now, I realise that some people do actually want to say that! But it's never a good idea to advertise to potential thieves. Even when you've put your device into a bag and away from prying eyes, remember that you could have been observed while doing so. So always keep those bags close at hand and never leave them unattended.

## Hugging-Mugging

One of the new types of criminal activity aimed at relieving you of your hard-earned smartphone is known as a *hugging-mugging*. Gangs of hugger-muggers target large groups of people celebrating events such as New Year's, Thanksgiving, or Christmas, or even people gathering at large-scale events such as the Olympics. In the attack, the hugger-muggers will pretend to be celebrating with you and your group, to the extent that they end up laughing, joking, and even dancing with you. This eventually leads to them making physical contact with you – maybe with an arm around your shoulder or waist. At this point, the attempt is made to rummage through your pockets or bag in order to obtain your smartphone, wallet, or keys to your car while other members of the gang will attempt to shield the attack.

Before you realise what has happened, the attack is over and the hugger-muggers have dispersed into the crowd looking for another victim. By the time you do realise that you are no longer in possession of your phone, purse, or wallet, you'll probably put it down to the fact that you mislaid or dropped it during the celebrations.

*When out and about, especially during celebrations, watch out for this type of attack. Be wary of people getting too close to you, and ensure that your smartphone is not just sitting in an easily accessible place.*

### The conveyor belt scam

So you're at the airport, waiting in line to put your bag containing your tablet computer through the x-ray machine. The two people ahead of you in the queue put their bags on the conveyor belt and so do you. The first person goes through, picks up his bags and disappears in the busy terminal. The second person has some sort of problem, resulting in the line being held up for a minute or two. By the time you get through, your bag containing your tablet is nowhere to be seen.

But what happened? Well, even though the two people in the queue appeared to be strangers, they were actually both part of the same scam team. While you were being held up by the second person, the first had already taken your bag and made off with it. Chances are your bag will be found not too far away, but minus anything of value – such as your tablet.

*When waiting to put your bags through the x-ray machine, wait until the way through is clear before putting anything on the conveyor belt. If there are a number of items already on the belt, wait for them to be claimed at the other end before putting your items through.*

### Screen guards

How many times have you been using your smartphone or tablet on the train when you sense the person next to you staring intently at your screen? You might shift uncomfortably in your seat while tilting your device so that they can no longer see, but this just exposes your screen more to the person on your other side. If the information on your device is sensitive, or private consider using a screen-guard. These are special polarising filters that fit over your screen (much like a screen protector that you put on your phone to stop the screen from being scratched.) but which restrict the view so that you can only see the screen properly if you're looking at it directly from in front. Anyone attempting to look at your screen from the side (for example the person sitting next to you on your plane, train, or coach) simply sees a black screen.

## Safety First

This section wouldn't be complete without some general safety tips. When traveling, many people do things that they wouldn't normally do back home and so while some of this may be common sense, it's still worthwhile highlighting.

- Don't make or receive calls while driving. It's probably against the law and is extremely dangerous, especially when you add in the factors of you being in an unfamiliar car, driving in an unfamiliar location. If you have to take a call, pull over, be brief, and carry on with your journey. Once you've got to your destination, finish the conversation.

- Don't send SMS/text messages while driving. Again, it's dangerous and probably against the law.

- Put frequently called numbers into speed dial. Most phones allow you to set up a favourites or speed dial list. Ensure that you do this prior to leaving so that you can contact friends and family quickly and with the minimum of fuss.

- Ensure that you know the relevant country codes. Many smartphones will work this out for you if you tell them your location but to be on the safe side, make sure that you know the international dialling codes for your home country and the country you are visiting. Every country is assigned what's known as an 'exit code' which is what is used when dialling outside of that particular country. So to call a number back home, you'll need to know the exit code for the country you are visiting. In addition, every country is assigned a country code, which is the code you use to dial in to your home country. Lastly, you'll need the telephone number you wish to call. Put it all together and you dial:

- Origin country exit code + destination country code + telephone number.

Now that we've covered the basics, let's have a more detailed look of how not to use your smartphone.

# Lesson 3: It's just a phone!

*"How in the world are people going to steal my money — or my identity — through my phone? I mean, what are the chances of that really happening? I just don't believe it's possible; After all   it's not a computer! It's just a phone!"*

Gone are the days when a phone was just a phone. Back in the nineties my phone of choice was a blue Nokia 5100. I loved that phone because it simply worked; it made calls. It received calls. And that's what a phone is supposed to do, right?

It did SMS, too which was pretty cool back then. It didn't have a camera. But that wasn't a problem because its 5-line, LCD screen wasn't capable of displaying pictures anyway. And hey, I could play snakes on the thing! That was real cutting edge stuff at the time.

But to put it simply, my Nokia did exactly what it said on the tin. It was a well-designed phone with good battery life that kept me in touch with others. No need to worry about viruses, identity theft, or getting hacked. Leave all of that malarkey to my PC!

Fast forward to September 2011, a report by UK telecoms regulator Ofcom showed that nearly one in three adults in the UK now uses a smartphone. Apple's iPhone was identified in the report as being the most popular; however teenagers (like my two) seemed to favour RIM's BlackBerry devices due to their popular BBM (BlackBerry Messenger) instant messaging services.

Indeed, the summer riots that engulfed London and other parts of the UK in 2011 were orchestrated in part by BBM; teenagers would message each other in closed groups, enabling them to co-ordinate and plan which centres to rob and stores to loot away from prying eyes. In fact David Cameron, the Prime Minister of the UK at the time, considered shutting down the BBM service as part of his measures to contain the spread of rioting.

If there ever was a top ten list of how not to use your smartphone, organising a riot would be way up there.

Internet usage on handhelds has mushroomed over the last two or three years with, not surprisingly, FaceBook leading the pack of popular online destinations with a staggering 43 million hours spent there by UK users in December 2010 alone.

Figures like these show us that smartphones are definitely here to stay. They have become much more affordable and, therefore, accessible to a much wider spectrum of users. And as well as them becoming more affordable and accessible with each year that passes, they also become more powerful and feature packed.

Used wisely, smartphones are ultra-useful and amazingly adaptable – they can be used to book your theatre tickets, check your bank balance, read a book, *write* a book, listen to music, watch movies, catch up on news, the list is endless.

Oh yes; they make calls too.

However, use your smartphone incorrectly, and you're potentially letting yourself in for a world of pain.

A while back my sister-in-law, Ruby, took the plunge and bought an iPhone. She loves it! All that pinch-to-zoom stuff has really got her hooked. However it wasn't long before she wanted my help as she was having problems understanding how to set up her calendars correctly.

"Sure!" I said. "No problem". So I had a look. Immediately I saw that she didn't have a passcode set; as soon as I slid the slider to unlock I was looking at the last app she had used – which just happened to be her email.

This didn't look good to me.

Now, the chances are that over 50% of people reading this book would have lost a phone at some point or another. I know I have. And it sucks. In fact, it *really* sucks. I explained to Ruby about the importance of setting a passcode just in case the unthinkable happens; maybe you're travelling on the London Underground and when it's time to get off you leave the train – and your phone – behind.

If something like this happens, and your smartphone then gets into the wrong hands, you want to make it as difficult as possible for someone to gain access to your information. And a passcode is your first line of defence.

In Ruby's case, my nephew (her son) had also set up shortcuts for her on her home screen so that she could easily get into her online banking and other websites that she used frequently.

This was starting to look ugly.

I showed Ruby how I was able to access her FaceBook account, update her status, and even change her password in order to lock her out if she tried to log on from another computer. I showed her how I could send & read email from her account, read her notes, and that I was able to access her photos too.

When she left some time later not only was she a calendar-whizz but her iPhone was much more secure, and so her *personal information* was much more secure.

Yes we'd set up a passcode, but that wasn't the only thing; I'd also raised her awareness of the threats that follow every smartphone user from the moment they open the box and power up their new device. I also armed her with practical advice and knowledge that she could implement to mitigate her exposure to those threats.

**What would anyone want with MY data?!**

Rest assured; the bad guys will find a use for it. Think about the spammers who send out hundreds of thousands of spam emails every day to random recipients. They realise that the vast majority of those emails will most likely get deleted or blocked by the anti-spam programs that the recipient or their Internet service provider has installed. The spammers also know that, of the emails that do get through, only a very small minority of recipients will actually open them and act on their contents. But for the spammers, that small minority is enough. Which is why they continue to spam, of course.

So, in a similar vein, the bad guys also realise and accept that only a small number of users that they target will bear fruit. But, as with the spammers, that small minority is enough.

Your mission, should you choose to accept it, is to ensure that you do not become one of these users who bear fruit.

Who would have thought that the smartphone you have in your pocket (or even the smartphone that you're reading this book on) could make you a victim of identity theft, fraud, or much more serious crimes?

Many people buy a smartphone because the slick marketing campaigns tell them they'll be able to surf the web, pick up email, hook up with friends, and tweet, post, and poke with the minimum of fuss and maximum of enjoyment.

While much of this is true, you should never lose sight of the fact that, just like laptops and desktop computers, smartphones and tablets have a much less savoury side to them which can turn around and bite you in the butt if the device isn't used with due care and attention.

This is mainly because the bad guys (the hackers who like doing bad things such as accessing your bank account without your permission) are always looking for new ways of duping and scamming people out of their money. And unsuspecting smartphone users like you are a fantastic opportunity. The bad guys employ many different tactics to achieve their goals; from the fake Wi-Fi networks as described in the Preface, to what is fast becoming their favourite method: malicious apps.

Let's get this straight – the only way for your smartphone or tablet to be totally secure is for you to leave it sitting in its sealed box with Wi-Fi and Bluetooth disabled, ensuring that your device is not connected to any type of network. But it wouldn't be much of a smartphone if it's stuck in a box would it?

So you're about to unbox your new device, power up, set up your email, get online, and download some apps. Follow the lessons in this book first to understand where the dangers are and how you can guard against them.

### Identity theft facts

Identity theft is one of the fastest growing crimes in many countries around the world. For example, in America there were more than 15 million victims in 2011.

Quite simply, identity theft, also known as identity fraud, occurs when the bad guys steal your personal information and impersonate you in order to buy goods or services, obtain information that only you should be privy to, or to commit a crime in your name.

Personal information is simply information that specifically defines you – for example your name, address, national insurance number, social security number, bank account numbers, credit card numbers, etc.

To obtain this information, identity thieves tend to prefer one of two approaches:

- Some identity thieves like to target you. Their objective is to take assets, mainly financial, from you – maybe by gaining control of your bank account through your computer or smartphone.

- Some identity thieves like to target others while impersonating you. Their objective is to obtain assets such as loans or credit cards in your name.

Neither of these is a good thing. You could end up in trouble with the law and your credit score will very likely be affected which means that when you need a legitimate loan, you won't be able to secure one.

So can you really become a victim of identity theft through your smartphone or tablet? Absolutely. On the traditional computer, hackers have found it relatively easy to target unsuspecting users and make money from them. Normally this happens through so-called 'client side' attacks where a weakness (often called a 'vulnerability') in a web browser such as Internet Explorer is exploited by the hacker in order to compromise the computer. In plain English, this just means that the bad guys look for loopholes in popular programs which they can use to gain access to the computer without the user realising.

While the web browser is a popular target for these vulnerabilities, other applications which have not been updated (or 'patched') to the latest version, such as Adobe Reader or Flash, can also be targeted.

While it's true that most smartphones and tablets are susceptible to being hacked, some are more susceptible than others. This is mainly down to the design of the Operating System (the set of programs that enable your device to function, play music, take pictures, etc.).

For example, when you compare a device running Google's Android Operating System, with another running Apple's iOS, you'll be struck by their similarities. However, closer inspection will highlight major differences in the implementation of these devices:

- iOS is a so-called 'closed' platform which imposes strict restrictions on the apps that developers can write for, and run on, it. In addition, apps for iOS devices can only be obtained and installed via Apple's iTunes Store. The closed nature of iOS frustrates some users who would like to have more control over what they run on their device. This has led to the practice of Jailbreaking. See Lesson 7 for more details on this.

- Android, on the other hand, is an 'open' platform. It provides the user with much more control over their device and the types of apps they can install to it. In addition Android also allows the 'side loading' of apps where users can bypass the official Android store and, instead, download and install apps from developer's websites or other sources. Of course, like many things, this is a double-edged sword; Android's popularity and openness make it a much more desirable target for hackers and identity thieves.

### Criminals follow crowds

It goes without saying that the more popular a computer system is, the more inviting it appears to hackers and cyber-criminals. We've seen this all before with computer viruses where the more widely-used Windows computers had many, many more times the amount of viruses than Macs did. Therefore, taking these things into account, Android devices are more at risk of being hacked than iOS devices. And Windows Phone 7 and Blackberry devices come somewhere in between.

The sheer popularity of smartphones and tablets leaves criminals with rich, and sometimes easy, pickings. Recent figures show that new-device activations for the iOS and Android platforms grew from an average of 1.5 million per day during the first three weeks of December 2011 to 6.8 million devices on Christmas Day - a whopping 353% increase. Compare that to a total of 2.8 million new-devices activations on 25th December 2010 to get an idea of how fast the market is growing. To the bad guys, this is a massive opportunity.

But fear not. No matter which device you're currently using, slight changes to your behaviour will make a world of difference and help to ensure that you get the absolute best out of your purchase with the minimum of risk.

## QR Codes

When you're out and about, have you ever wondered what those funny square barcodes are that you see popping up all over the place? If you're not sure what I'm talking about, they look like this:

You see them in magazine adverts, bus shelters, on the tube or metro, at the theatre, literally all over the place. They're called **Quick Response Codes** but are more commonly known as QR Codes. The idea behind QR Codes is great: You simply point your smartphone or tablet at them and scan them in the same way that your groceries get scanned when you're out shopping. Then, miraculously, your device shows you more information about the product or service that the QR code was attached to. Simple!

In fact, it's not really miraculous. In most cases the QR Code simply contains a website address. So when you scan it, your smartphone simply takes you to that website and shows you the relevant promotion or information.

But not so fast - while QR Codes are great, and a really convenient way of getting information about goods or services, they can also be extremely dangerous. You see, when you scan them, you're essentially using them blind.

When you look at a QR code such as the one above, what do you see? A square with a bunch of patterns that could mean absolutely anything. Even if it is just a website address, you can't tell it's a website address. The QR Code is smartphone-readable sure, but it's definitely not human-readable, and this means that the advert or poster containing the QR code can say it does one thing, (like claim to give you free stuff or a great deal), but in reality when scanned it can take you somewhere quite unexpected such as a hacked, cracked, or compromised website which can then proceed to infect your computer, tablet, or smartphone with malware.

And you can't tell just by looking at it; at least with a traditional website address you have a fighting chance of seeing where the link will take you before you click on it.

Some bad guys have been known to print QR codes to their own compromised or virus-infected websites and stick the QR Code over legitimate QR Codes on posters in the subway, or at bus shelters. This trick catches out a lot of people; they see the advert for a product that interests them and then scan the QR Code that the bad guys have stuck on top of the legitimate one. As soon as the code is scanned and the compromised website is opened, the device can potentially become infected.

So if you haven't guessed already, be wary of QR codes. Especially QR Codes that look like they have been stuck on or altered in some way. Generally, QR Codes printed in magazine adverts or other professionally produced publications or documentation will be safe to use, however use caution when scanning codes if you are out and about.

If you have any doubts, instead of using the QR code, just open your browser and find the product on the internet yourself. It won't be that hard and will be safer than scanning a code you're unsure of.

Now that you know all about QR Codes, try scanning the code on the previous page to get some **free** Apple stuff!

And just so that you know, the code above will take you to the *How NOT To Books* website here: http://www.hownottobooks.info/index.php/free-stuff

**NOTE:** Some devices come with a QR Code reader built-in. If yours doesn't, you might need to download a QR Code reader app from your favourite app store.

**What not to do**

- Don't make the mistake of thinking that your smartphone is just a phone. It's not.

- Don't leave your Bluetooth in discover mode. If you have Bluetooth connectivity, set it to non-discoverable mode when you are not using it.

- Don't leave Bluetooth enabled if you're not using it. Disabling Bluetooth will make your device that little bit more secure and you'll save battery life, too!

- Don't underestimate the importance of your PIN/passcode. It's your first line of defence and, at a minimum, will stop people being able to snoop at your messages and other data without you knowing.

- Don't scan every QR Code you see. As an alternative, browse to the website for the product manually.

- Don't use your smartphone to organise and co-ordinate riots. It's just not cool.

# Lesson 4: Apps, apps, and more apps!

*"I keep hearing about apps. Apps for this. Apps for that. Seems like there's an app for almost everything! But what actually are apps? Are they safe? And where can I download them from?"*

Depending on your smartphone or tablet of choice, you'll most likely want to hook it up to the Internet and download as many apps as you can as soon as you've powered it up. What's a smartphone without apps, after all?

But wait just a moment – how do you know that the apps you're after are safe to download?

## Apps 101

Let's get to grips with what an app actually is. First, let's get this straight. Apps are nothing new. Google's successful Apps suite of online services which include webmail, calendars, etc. first saw the light of day in 2002. However lately, the term has been hijacked by Apple's marketing machine and has become synonymous with the programs that run on Apple's iPhone, iPad, and iPod touch. When we refer to apps in this eBook, we mean mobile apps in general. In other words, we're referring to apps that run on a wide variety of smartphones and tablet devices and not specifically iPhone apps.

Put simply, an app is a smartphone or tablet application that *does something*. As the shortened name implies, apps typically have less functionality than the 'grown up' applications that run on desktop computers or laptops. For example, an email app running on a smartphone might allow you to send and receive email (as you might expect) and even create folders so that you can move and organize your mail neatly, but it probably won't provide you with the advanced features found in a desktop email application such as rules and smart folders which enable you to organize your mail to an even greater degree.

So apps usually take the form of 'cut down' versions of the more mature desktop applications.

## What types of apps are there?

There is a wide, and growing, spectrum of apps available. Some apps are pretty cool, some are pretty useful, and some are pretty useless (unless 'farting' apps are a must-have for you). Some apps are just pretty. And, of course, some apps have been hit with the ugly stick. But mixed among them are apps that are out to get your data, snoop in your private affairs, and generally stick their digital noses where they have no business sticking them.

For example a while back a programmer produced an app that promised to give the user an exclusive sneak peek at the (as yet unreleased) latest Twilight movie. (For those of you who have been living in a cave recently, Twilight is an extremely successful series of vampire novels that have been turned into movies). Understandably, many Android users rushed to download the app in order to get the exclusives on the new movie before anyone else. Unfortunately for them, the app wasn't all that it seemed; after being installed, the app would send the user's contact details to an address on the Internet where the programmer was then able to retrieve it. Contact information is a mine of useful data for identity thieves – by viewing the contacts of a business user for example, they can see prospective and current clients, suppliers and other sensitive data.

Now – during the installation of that app, it *requested* access to the user's contacts. Alarm bells should have started ringing for the users at that time; why would the app need to have access to the contact details of their friends and relatives? For the ones who decided to decline the application's request to access their contacts their information was safe.

However, for the others who chose to grant the app the permissions that it requested, they may as well have said goodbye to their data as the app was then able to send this information to the developer as soon as it was launched.

Being smart in your choice of apps and the way in which you use them will pay dividends. Being ignorant in your choice of apps and the way in which you use them will also pay dividends! Unfortunately, those dividends won't be for you; the individuals who write these apps are the ones that will benefit, mainly at your cost.

There are a lot of apps available in a lot of different genres. Here are some of the more popular types:

- Business

- Education

- Entertainment
- Finance
- Games
- Health & Fitness
- Lifestyle
- Medical
- Music
- Navigation
- News
- Photography
- Productivity
- Reference
- Social Networking
- Sport
- Travel
- Utilities

These are just top-level categories to give you an example; there are many more sub-categories available, all crammed with apps. But notice none of the categories are called *Bad* or *Dangerous*. (And no, I'm not referring to Michael Jackson albums here). App stores typically list and organise the apps they sell via these top-level categories.

## What's an App store?

Before Apple introduced the iPhone back in 2007, the concept of an App store as we know it today didn't really exist. Prior to the iPhone, if you had a smartphone and you wanted to install a program onto it, you had to visit the software developer's website, purchase the program, download it to your computer, and then transfer it to your device. Because App Stores provide a central place to obtain your apps from, they're a good thing. From a security point of view, App stores generally give you the following:

- A secure place to buy – an App store (like the one run by Apple) provides users with a safe and secure location from where they can purchase and download apps. In Apple's case the apps are vetted by the

App store guardians at Apple; only safe apps that are not buggy are allowed onto the App store. Any apps that are deemed to be a security risk or not suitable for other reasons, are denied a listing on the store. For example, Apple will not allow an Entertainment app on the App store if that app tries to access your contacts. Because why would an Entertainment app want to access your contacts in the first place? There's no legitimate reason, and so the app would be rejected. It's not fool-proof and things may slip through the net, but it's a good line of defence against hackers.

- Impartial Reviews – one of the great things about an App store is that you will find impartial ratings and reviews from other users for each of the apps on sale. This means that you're less likely to be swayed by the developer's bold, and sometimes misleading, descriptions that may be present on their own website or online store. In addition, any security risks or concerns with apps will be visible here as users provide their feedback. Take this reviews seriously and avoid apps which have bad comments or low star rankings.

- Standards – a developer can create an app over a weekend and put it up for sale on his or her website with little, or no, checking for bugs and other issues. In contrast some (not all) App stores are regulated. This means that for an app to reach the 'for sale' stage on the store, it must have passed a number of tests and conditions. While having guidelines such as these in place will help ensure that the apps you purchase from the store don't both suck and blow at the same time, be aware that some will *still* suck.

Users download a lot of apps – for example, in early December 2011, the Android store reached the milestone of 10 billion downloads. Apple, announced 15 billion downloads in July 2011 – staggering amounts. Amazingly, the pace is increasing and by the second half of 2012, Android is expected to have overtaken iOS in terms of app downloads.

## Reviews

To re-iterate the point made above, before you download and install an app, it's a good idea to see if that app has any reviews and then make your decision based on them. Reviews are typically performed by people who have purchased the app so in most instances they are extremely useful. In fact, reviews are probably the single most important indicator when it comes to deciding what app you're going to put on your device next. Not only will reviews tell you if the app you're planning on downloading stinks, many will highlight any security concerns that the app may have.

## Should I only get apps from an App store?

This will depend on your smartphone or tablet. But in a word, yes. Apps that you install to your device should always come from trusted sources and App stores are a good bet because many of the apps on the store have been through a vetting process. Following on from the success of Apple's App store for its iPhone and other iOS devices, (iPod touch and iPad), many other companies have created their own App stores through which users of their devices can purchase apps. For example, Google have the Android Market which allows users of Android OS devices to obtain apps, Palm have the App Catalog, Microsoft has the Windows Marketplace, RIM has the BlackBerry App World, etc.

All smartphone or tablet vendors want their users to have a great experience while using their devices, and so the vendors try as much as possible to ensure that their App stores are easy to use and, more importantly, safe. This means that in most situations, the apps that you download will be safe. Note that I say *most* situations. More on this later.

The concept of an App store where users can easily obtain apps is, therefore, well proven and established so it makes sense that you should purchase your apps from an App store. Indeed, with some platforms, the App store is the *only* officially sanctioned way to get apps onto your device.

For example, Apple's App store app comes pre-installed on every single iPhone, iPod touch or iPad sold by the company and is the officially sanctioned way of getting apps onto one of these devices (the App Store can also be accessed via iTunes running on a Mac or PC).

### What's a web app?

There are two main types of app: *Web apps* and *Native apps*.

Native apps are the types we've mentioned above and are the most common type. A native app is an app that has been written specifically to run on a particular device. For example, a native iPhone app will only run on an iPhone - if you attempt to run it on another device it simply won't work. With a native app, the app is downloaded and stored permanently on the device, meaning that it's available for use at all times – even if there is no Internet connectivity.

Web apps are different. A web app is not downloaded or stored on the device, meaning that without an Internet connection, it is not possible to run the app.

Web apps are essentially websites which have been designed to mimic, or emulate, a native app in look and feel. As the web app is really a website, whenever you want to run the web app, you access it via the web browser on the device. An advantage of this approach is that most smartphones or tablets can access the web app, regardless of the OS, hardware, or firmware being used on the particular device.

A disadvantage is that many attacks carried out on users are achieved through bad websites. The bad guys set up a website which looks for weak spots in the user's browser, so when the user browses to the site, code is executed that tries to find 'exploits' or ways that the bad guys can access data on your device without you knowing.

In addition, the bad guys can 'compromise' a legitimate site. That is, they will hack the website and install their programs without the website owner realising. Again, when a user browses to the website, the bad guys' code is run in an attempt to gain access to the computer browsing the website. Some users may suspect something is wrong and try to browse to another site – but nine times out of ten the damage has already been some and the device is already compromised

As a web app is simply a website, so be aware that they can also be compromised in this way. If the website has an official native app, use that instead of the web app to minimise the potential of your device being compromised.

**Malicious Apps**

In addition to the native apps and web apps described above, the bad guys have found that they can pedal bad native apps with surprising ease. These bad (or malicious) apps typically take the form of a Trojan horse. A Trojan horse is, like the ancient Greek fable, something that purports to do one thing when, in reality, it aims to do something completely different. For example, a Trojan app may appear to be game and, when downloaded, it may actually provide you with a basic game experience. As the experience will very likely be poor, you'll remove the game shortly after and subsequently think little of it.

However, unknown to you, the Trojan code will have already been run and performed a number of different actions. For example:

- The Trojan may have already forwarded personal data from your phone on to the hackers.

- The Trojan might have changed the permissions and settings on your phone, making it easy for the hackers to access your phone remotely and without your knowledge.

- Alternatively, the Trojan might have compromised your tablet or smartphone by installing hidden programs. These hidden programs will be running constantly in the background of your device even after you've removed the 'game'. You won't be able to see them easily, (without the use of special utilities), however you may notice that your phone has become slower than normal as the hidden programs are taking up resources. These programs can perform a number of different actions and will generally be used to spy on your activities.

It goes without saying then that malicious apps – known collectively as 'malware' - are precisely the types of app that you do not want installed on your smartphone. Some malware even has the ability to remotely control your device – enabling the camera or turning on the microphone in order to take pictures or listen to your conversations. Commercial software is now available that allows hackers to quickly and easily monitor your phone conversations as well as your email conversations, read your messages, and even determine the room you are sitting in. And in most situations, you won't even know it's installed.

Worryingly, in the first half of 2011 malware on smartphones rose by over 30 percent. However as most computer security experts will tell you, the average user is oblivious to this fact and simply isn't concerned by smartphone malware and their threats, mainly because they have no idea what malware is and what it can do.

## Droid Dream

In March 2011, the bad guys uploaded 21 different malicious apps to Google's Android store. Over the next four days, those malicious apps were downloaded by unsuspecting users over 50,000 times!

The apps contained a Trojan that stole personal information from the user's phone such as their credit card info and address contact details. In addition, the app installed other malicious apps onto the user's phone without them knowing. This attack – known as the 'Droid Dream attack' - left many users exposed to identity, as well as financial, theft.

The Droid Dream attack is just one example of a malware attack on smartphones. This type of attack is on the increase and will only get worse in 2012 and beyond.

## The Big Red Button

Apple came in for some criticism when they announced that they were implementing a "*Big Red Button*" for apps sold on their App store.

Essentially, this meant that they had the power to remotely remove any dodgy apps from everyone's iPhone, iPod touch, and iPad, whenever they felt a need to. The idea being that if the bad guys managed to upload a malicious app to the App store and users managed to download it, Apple would be able to automatically remove the app from every iPhone/iPod touch/iPad that had installed it the next time that device went online.

Critics cried foul and stated that Apple was taking things a bit too far with this ability to remotely wipe apps that the user had paid for.

However, security-aware folk applauded the decision as it showed that Apple had thought seriously about security on the iPhone. But not only had they thought seriously about it, they had decided to implement an elegant solution to a potentially serious problem.

Google implemented a similar Big Red Button that, too, gave them the ability to remotely kill any errant apps that decided to do dodgy things on their user's Android device, and they were forced to use this feature after the Droid Dream attack took place – the app was automatically removed from any Android devices the next time those devices went online helping to minimize the effects of the attack.

**What not to do:**

- Don't download apps from unofficial websites. Wherever possible, purchase and download your apps from an official App store.

- Don't ignore reviews and feedback that others have left about an app. Their experiences with the app should guide your decisions regarding purchase and installation.

- Avoid using web apps – these can be compromised. If the website that you are visiting has an official native app, download and install that instead.

- When installing an app, don't grant it permissions just because it asks you.

- If your smartphone or tablet has become slow after you've installed and removed an app, don't just ignore it. Do some research on that particular app to determine if it may have contained a Trojan. At the first sign of trouble, restore your device back to factory settings.

# Lesson 5: Nosey Apps

*"So what's the big deal? I installed an app, it wanted to access my location and my contacts, and I said yes. I mean, it's only an app. I really don't see what the problem is."*

Some apps want to have their fingers in all the pies. And I'm not only talking Apple or Blackberry pies here. Android, Windows Phone 7, et al are pretty much the same.

As you'd expect, your smartphone is very personal to you, and so it naturally contains information, names, numbers, email addresses, etc. that are also very personal to you.

So why does that poker app that you just downloaded need to access this information? Why would it need to know about your contacts? Or insist on determining your location? Why does that app need to be so nosey?

## Location, Location, Location

Many real estate agents say that the three most important factors in determining the desirability of a property are *"location, location, location"*. Some app developers share the same thought when it comes to you, their customer.

Many smartphones or tablets come with a GPS function. Much in the same way as your TomTom or Garmin satellite navigation system works in your car, these systems use a number of outside hardware systems in order to establish the position of the device, down to an accuracy of a few meters. Smartphones and tablets also use cell towers and even wi-fi networks to triangulate the device's position.

## Maps

And this is great, right? I recently had to take my son to a friend's birthday party. I thought I knew the street address, but pretty soon I was driving in circles trying to work out where the house was located. Rather foolishly, I neglected to take my TomTom with me when we got in the car. Even though

I've been an iOS user from the very first iPhone, I hadn't really used the Maps app in anger and so after a frustrating ten minutes driving back and forth I guessed that this was good a time as any.

I whipped out my iPhone, fired up Maps, and waited for the system to find itself. Sure enough, within seconds I had a good set of directions to the other side of town; I'd been way off in where I thought the party was. But while this functionality lends itself well to the usefulness of the device, it can also be controversial...

### iPhone tracker

In the spring of 2011 two British software developers, Pete Warden and Alisdair Allan, released a program that purportedly showed how Apple were tracking the movements of iPhone users. The pair had been working on ways of visualising location data for websites by plotting locations extracted from databases. By downloading the program that they produced and installing it on your Mac, you could immediately see your last six month's movements plotted nicely on a graph before your very eyes. I was initially sceptical that it would work, and so I downloaded the program and installed it on my Mac. Sure enough, I could see how I had been travelling to and from my home in North West London to my place of work in Buckinghamshire, with occasional trips to East London where my mother lives, Luton where I have friends, and everything in between. To say I was gobsmacked is an understatement.

In the ensuing days, Apple got a lot of heat for this seemingly gross invasion of privacy. First, this was *Apple* keeping tabs on your movements – not some dodgy app developer trying his luck. But second, and possibly more worrying, what was being done with this information? Was it being sent to Apple on a regular basis? Were they storing it? And what would it be used for?

The furore continued to build up a head of steam, and Apple was forced to respond promptly in order to avoid the saga turning into a public relations disaster. The company provided a complete response, explaining that they were not tracking the location of users' phones, that they had never done so, and that they had no plans ever to do so.

### So what was it we were we able to see, then?

Apple stated that users' iPhones were simply maintaining a database of Wi-Fi hotspots and cell towers around the phone's current location to help your iPhone rapidly and accurately calculate its location when requested. Calculating a phone's location using just GPS satellite data can take up to several minutes. However, the iPhone reduces this time to just a few seconds by using Wi-Fi hotspot and cell tower data to quickly find GPS satellites.

Essentially the device was maintaining a database of nearby cell towers and Wi-Fi hotspots in order to help it determine its position faster and more accurately - a system I benefitted from while trying to get my son to his party. A by-product of this technique was that when the contents of that database were plotted on a map, it appeared to show all of the locations that the user had visited with their phone.

This was a plausible explanation, and it subsequently came to light that other platforms such as Android employed similar techniques. Apple has since updated iOS to enable this feature to be turned off by the user if required.

**They want to target you with ads!**

While Apple may not seem too concerned about tracking your location, the same cannot be said for many app developers. Many apps are ad-supported. This means that the app is free for you to download and use, but obviously the developer needs to make some money somehow. After all, he didn't stay up until 2am night after night developing his app just to give it away to you for free. He makes his money back by placing ads in the app and getting paid a small amount when someone clicks the ad and makes a purchase.

But for many ads to work properly, the app needs to know where you are. After all, there's no point in serving you ads for *Ponderosa Steakhouse* on Orlando's International Drive when you're actually walking down Wembley High Street in North London is there? So the incentive is there for the developer to accurately determine your location, thereby ensuring that you get served relevant ads.

This is one of the reasons why apps that have no business knowing your location will prompt you to grant them those permissions when the app is installed.

The first thing you have to realise is that you do **not** have to grant an app permissions to access your location just because it requests it. For some apps, location awareness is essential for them to function correctly; for example a navigation app, or an app that recommends nearby attractions or events. But why does an app that lets you play sudoku want to know where you are at this precise moment in time?

The answer, of course, is: it doesn't. So when it pops up that dialog asking for permissions to access your location, just say No.

**Find My Friends**

With the release of iOS 5 in October 2011, Apple released an app called Find My Friends. As its name implies, the app allows friends who are using iOS devices (iPod touch, iPhone and iPad) to locate each other on a map. Great! You can use it to make hooking up with friends much easier, or even to ensure that your kids have got home safely from school assuming they have one of the supported devices.

Of course, it's consensual – meaning that for you to track your friends or family, they need to accept your tracking request, and you'll need to accept their tracking request so that they can track you.

But hang on a moment. Do you really want your friends to know where you are every minute of every day? Sure, there is the option to temporarily hide yourself from your 'followers' but in practice, will you really remember to flick that switch? People install an app, enable a few settings, close the app and forget about it all the time; why should Find My Friends be any different?

What happens if you've let your boy/girlfriend track your location. Then, months later you break up. Will you really remember to turn off their ability to know where you are every minute of every day?

Therefore if you decide to use this feature, remember to disable it after use unless you don't mind your location being tracked.

## Geotagging

When you take a picture and post it up to Flickr or FaceBook did you know that people who view that picture can see exactly where it was taken? They can plot it quite easily using services like Google Maps to see exactly where your photo was taken. Obviously, this means that if you take a picture and post, blog, or tweet it immediately, you're also posting, blogging, or tweeting your location at the same time – making it easy for someone to keep tabs on you. This is made possible by another feature that might be perceived as an invasion of privacy called 'geotagging'. This feature is present on many modern smartphones and cameras and works because those devices have built-in GPS features. Whenever a picture is taken, a geotag (essentially the current latitude and longitude of the device taking the picture) is attached to the picture, enabling its location to be determined.

## Find My (Boy)Friends

Shortly after the release of Apple's iPhone 4S, a story emerged about a female whose husband had given her one of the new phones with Find My Friends already installed and enabled. Crucially, the husband had made a tracking request from his iPhone and had accepted it on his wife's new iPhone before he gave it to her. He had suspected her of having an affair and so he wanted to keep track of her whereabouts. Sure enough, one evening she told him she was at one of her girlfriend's houses in New York's East Village, whereas Find My Friends told him she was on the other side of town – specifically at the home of the man he suspected she was having the affair with.

The moment he found out that his wife was cheating, the husband posted his story and screenshots from his iPhone on the forums of the popular website Macrumors. Posting under the name of Thomas Metz, he explained how he'd used the app to catch his wife out and that he'd be divorcing her. He signed off his post by saying "thankfully, she's the rich one".

The story then grew legs and was featured on Fox News, the Yahoo World News Headlines, and numerous other websites.

It has never been determined whether this was a hoax or a real story. Either way, it doesn't take a great stretch of the imagination to see that scenarios similar to this will be played out many, many more times as these types of tracking apps become more pervasive.

### Find My Killer

Having second thoughts about granting apps permissions to track your location?

If not, maybe the sad, disturbing, and definitely real-life story of Mark G. Woodland will change your mind. Mr. Woodland was a gay man who used a social networking iPhone app specifically designed to help gays hook up. The app works by each user building a profile of themselves that includes a picture, likes and dislikes, etc. When the app is running it looks out for other users of the app who have also created a profile and are nearby. Interested parties can contact each other to chat online or arrange to meet up.

While the idea might initially seem harmless and just a bit of fun, it can also have extremely serious repercussions. On April 24, 2010 Mark Woodland arranged a date after hooking up with Tommy McKey Reed, another user of the app. They met up a few hours later.

Later that same day Mr. Woodland's badly beaten and stabbed body was found in his apartment by his roommate who had returned home after being out for the day.

Within a very short space of time, police were able to identify a suspect and make an arrest. By examining the victim's iPhone, police were quickly able to establish that Mr. Woodland had arranged a date via the app and were able to track down Tommy Reed by his username and other details in his profile. In addition, eyewitnesses provided descriptions of the last man to be seen with Mr. Woodland – and those descriptions matched Tommy Reed who was subsequently booked on charges of second-degree murder.

On October 14, 2011 20-year-old Tommy McKey Reed was sentenced to life imprisonment for the murder of Mark G. Woodland.

While this may be an extreme case, it highlights the dangers of sharing your location with strangers

## Granting permissions

As we've seen, many apps that you install to your device want to determine your location, access your contacts, or do something similar with your private information. However, before they can access this information, they need to be granted the relevant permissions.

If you grant a bad app system-level permissions, your device is compromised. This means that the app (and, by proxy, the developer of the app) now has some form of control over your device that he shouldn't do.

So think carefully before you grant permissions; does that utility app really need to know your location? Really?

Here are some permissions that malicious apps can trick users into granting unnecessarily:

- **Make phone calls** – When would you ever want an app to make phone calls? Well, some do legitimately (such as Google Voice) but be wary of any app requesting this permission as the app will very likely end up calling premium numbers.

- **Send SMS or MMS** – Don't allow in most cases. Again, premium txt numbers can apply.

- **Read/Write Contact data** – Some social networking apps might legitimately do this, but beware of granting this permission.

- **Read Calendar** – See above.

- **Read Browser History** – does the app really need to see which websites you've been visiting? Don't grant this permission if you don't believe it does.

- **Fine (GPS)/Coarse (Network) location** – Granting this permission will allow the app to keep track of your location. Only grant for apps that obviously require this.

- **Create Bluetooth connection** – This might be legitimate for some file sharing, or transfer apps. If your app doesn't perform this type of function, do not grant this permission.

- **Full Internet access** – Most malware needs internet access in order to function. Disable this if you believe your app does not need this functionality.

- **Manage accounts** – Speaks for itself. Do you want another app to manage accounts on your device?

- **Use Credentials** – Again, this allows an app to impersonate you. Not clever.

- **Install Packages** - Allows the app to install other apps onto your device. Only apps that obviously need to do this (like Amazon market) need this permission. Other apps that request this permission are apps you'll want to avoid.

- **Modify Global System Settings** – Oh *hell* no!

- **Take pictures & video** – Be wary of this one – especially on apps that are not video/picture related.

## Sloppy developers

A while back I installed an app that grabbed a lot of headlines due to its fantastic design and user interface. It's undeniably cool as it provides you with a magazine-style view of all things important to you - from your FaceBook contacts and their activity, to Twitter feeds from people you're following, as well as news stories from the categories that you choose to follow. All very slick and extremely well put together.

However, when setting up the FaceBook component, I barely noticed a message flash up on my iPad's screen: "*Access my data when I'm not using the application*".

But Dang it! I was too eager to see what everyone was talking about and pressed "OK" before I really should have done. And, if that happened to me, I'm sure it's also happened to lots of other users of the app eager to put it through its paces.

Now, call me paranoid, but I don't see why apps should be able to poke around in my data like that! Also, a lot of times, I install an app, play with it for a while and then never open it again. Even if I chose never to access that app again after today, it would still be poking around in my stuff!

But it gets worse; after hunting high and low, there was no way I could see in the app to actually turn this feature off!

Not good.

I poked around even more, carried out some Google searches, and found that to turn this feature off, you need to access FaceBook. That's right: to turn off that feature in the app, I had to log into FaceBook and do it from there in the following way:

1. Log in to FaceBook and click **Account.**

2. Click **Application Settings.**

3. The app that I installed on my iPad is listed here. Click **Edit Settings.**

4. Click **Additional Permissions.**

5. Un-check **Access my data when I'm not using the application.**

6. Click **Okay.**

The reason I've given you the steps above is to encourage you to check your settings if you're a FaceBook user; if other apps that you use (whether on your smartphone, tablet, or through a website) are configured to access your personal data, you'll see them here. And if you'd rather that app didn't have access to your data, un-check the option.

With the plethora of Social Networking sites and apps, users are sharing info about themselves that they don't know they're sharing. And it's all too easy to get caught up in it all.

A quick note to app developers: Please allow your users to easily enable and disable privacy-related features directly in the app. You've made an awesome product, so please don't turn people off with a lack of consideration of their privacy needs.

**What not to do:**

- Don't ignore the settings. When you install an app, check its settings to make sure it's doing what you think it's doing.

- Don't forget to periodically check which apps are accessing your location.

- Don't forget to periodically check which users have access to your location.

- Don't store things like bankcard PIN numbers, passwords, etc. under obvious names in your contacts. If you have to do this, make sure you hide them sufficiently so that if your contact data is compromised, it won't be obvious to the bad guys what the information is.

- Don't allow apps to install other apps because you have no control over what they're installing.

## Lesson 6: Public Wi-Fi Hotspots

*"Oh goody! This coffee shop has a wireless Wi-Fi hotspot. Now I can check my bank to see if the money I'm waiting on has come through. Online banking is pretty safe nowadays so there shouldn't be a problem, right? I mean, it's not as though I'm risking anything! Right?!"*

You'd be surprised at just what you are risking. Like many people who use mobile devices, on more than one occasion you've probably whipped out your smartphone or tablet and seen a login window to a WI-Fi hotspot appear. That comes as no surprise because Wi-Fi networks are extremely commonplace now – many coffee shops and burger outlets now offer free Wi-Fi as an incentive to visit their establishment. And they can be extremely useful when you're out and about and need to check your email, catch up with your friends on FaceBook, or post that quick update to Twitter.

But before you connect, think carefully. Exactly how secure is that hotspot? And what dangers might there be lurking within? Is it a real, legitimate hotspot or have the bad guys simply set up a honey pot with the intention of sniffing as many passwords and other credentials as they can? (A honey pot is a fake resource set up by cyber criminals in order to trap unsuspecting users. The honey pot is made appealing to the end user to encourage them to access it).

Remember the man-in-the-middle attack story in the Preface of this book? Well, that type of attack is very real, and it catches out many people, including the relative I mentioned. In his case, he had flown over to New York on a business trip and planned to stay in a hotel there for just a few days. Within a week of getting back home he had started getting application letters and forms being delivered to his home. After checking up with the financial institutions that had sent the letters, it quickly became obvious that someone had got hold of his details and was actively using them to apply for loans and credit cards.

He immediately suspected the Wi-Fi that he had been using the previous week, and contacted the hotel who confirmed his fears: they didn't provide Wi-Fi for guests; whatever network he was connecting to was not provided by the hotel.

In his case he was lucky that he'd discovered the problem relatively early, and so he was able to take the necessary steps to minimize the potential of the identity theft by placing a fraud alert on his credit report. This would stop the bad guys from being able to open more accounts in his name as the fraud report would show up when the relevant company ran a credit check on him before opening the account, (see *Lesson 1: First things first* for more information on who to contact to set up a fraud alert).

Unfortunately, not everyone is this lucky – in many cases it takes months before any wrongdoing comes to light – and by that time, a lot of damage may already have been done, both to your financials and your reputation.

### So why are hotspots so dangerous?

Whenever you connect to someone else's Wi-Fi from your smartphone or tablet, your personal data is *vulnerable* to hackers. You won't *definitely* get hacked, but the *potential* is there. Remember: you're accessing the Internet, downloading email, and updating FaceBook, over someone else's Internet connection. Who knows how they have it configured?

While there are many legitimate Wi-Fi hotspots around that are perfectly safe to use, there are also many that can cause you a whole heap of trouble. If you frequent locations such as airport lounges, coffee shops, convention centres, libraries, and other public places, you'll already have seen the proliferation of hotspots that are available for you to connect to. However, some of these should be referred to as danger spots as well as hotspots; because of their popularity, they are frequently targeted by the bad guys because they know that the chances are high they'll be able to connect to an unsuspecting user's computer, or trick unsuspecting users into connecting to their Wi-Fi hotspots.

If you have no alternative but to connect to a public Wi-Fi network or hotspot, practice safe surfing on every occasion:

The first and most important thing to do is make sure that the network that you are connecting to is genuine and not something that's been thrown up by criminals intent on getting your personal information. Before you connect to a hotspot, speak to a nearby receptionist or individual who would know to attempt to confirm that the hotspot is legitimate. Also, look out for signs; most organisations that provide free Wi-Fi will generally post up a sign advertising the fact. The sign will contain the network name (also known as the SSID) and password. If you can't see a sign, and there are no individuals around to confirm that the network is legitimate, don't join it.

Avoid Wi-Fi networks that do not require a password to join. Running a Wi-Fi hotspot competently and professionally means taking security seriously. A major indication that security has taken a back seat is where the hotspot has been so poorly configured such that it doesn't even need a password to connect to it. This could be because the individual who set it up was simply incompetent, or misguidedly thought he was making it 'easier' for people to connect by removing the need for a password. Even if the hotspot is legitimate, hackers who have identified the fact that no password is required to connect will find it easier poke around in places where they are not wanted. Another alternative is that the insecure hotspot was actually set up by identity thieves wanting people to connect to their network. If you've ever connected to a hotspot that didn't require a password and then felt smug that you've somehow beaten the system, think twice before patting yourself on the back: If a password is not required, the network is not safe. And connecting to Wi-Fi networks that are not safe is a very bad idea.

If you've confirmed that the hotspot is legitimate and you've connected to it, feel free to surf to your heart's content, but under no circumstances should you perform any financial transactions over it. This covers buying things from popular online destinations as well as accessing your bank account. While the hotspot may be genuine, you still cannot guarantee that the bad guys are not eavesdropping to see if they can glean information being sent between your device and their network. If you limit the value of this information there will be nothing for the bad guys to steal. Bottom line: If the Wi-Fi network is not your own, wait until you get to a network that you really trust (like your home network) before conducting financial transactions. If you need to check your bank balance, visit an ATM instead; you'd be surprised at the features modern ATMs have.

Restrict your surfing to general websites that don't require you to provide account details or other log in credentials. While it's true that cyber criminals are after your banking details, they'll quite happily take any other personal details that you care to share with them such as logins to your email accounts, etc. Essentially, you want to eliminate the potential of any of your passwords or personal information being sent over the W-Fi connection. It's not as easy as it sounds though, especially when you remember that most browsers will auto-fill your credentials into some websites when you visit them. Be alert when visiting those sites.

Once the bad guys have you on their network, they can then redirect you to websites that look legitimate, but are really just elaborate fakes. Those websites then attempt to download and run malware on your smartphone or tablet. If they are successful, and the malware is run, then your device becomes compromised. When your device is compromised in this way the bad guys can access it through a 'back door' which the malware opens up.

The back door allows the criminals to run programs and code on your device whenever they want to. Typically the programs will allow the criminals to snoop around your device and access your personal data, take pictures and even record audio and video. If they have downloaded your data they can then use that data for their own means, or sell it on to other identity thieves.

### Poorly configured hotspots

Not all Wi-Fi hotspots set out to grab your data or compromise your smartphone. Some might be legitimate, but the individual who set the network up was incompetent. The result is an insecure hotspot which is more likely to make you end up with a compromised device after using it.

Many people set up Wi-Fi networks without changing the default administrator passwords. Hackers who are skilled enough (and have the right equipment) can tell what type of hardware is being used on the network. They can then try the default passwords for those bits of hardware (such as routers) and, chances are, they'll be logged on with administrator permissions in no time. Once they have control of the network, they can make changes to their benefit and to the detriment of anyone who logs onto the network.

For example, the hacker may turn off encryption, meaning that information sent over the network – such as passwords and banking information - is sent in plain text. This makes the information easy for the bad guys to access and is one of the reasons why you should not visit banking or financial websites over Wi-Fi hotspots.

Once the bad guys have the network how they want it, all they need to do is sit back and observe. Sooner or later they will have someone logging on and accessing sites that require passwords and other confidential data which can be harvested for later use.

In addition, when using public Wi-Fi, look out for shoulder surfers. These are people who'll look over your shoulder to see your passwords and account names as you type them. While you may not think they'll be able to see much, you'll be surprised; they have become very skilled at working out what you're typing.

In addition to shoulder surfing, identity thieves have been known to use cameras with powerful zoom lenses in order to record passwords and keystrokes. Bear these points in mind when choosing your seat.

### On the other side

There's another side to public hotspots; the people that serve them.

Increasingly, that could be me or you. For example, companies such as British Telecom or Virgin Media in the UK will provide you with equipment which lets you share your high-speed connection through an access point. Effectively, users can then access the Internet through your connection.

Making your Internet connection available to the public through a WI-FI hotspot could pay handsomely – the providers offer numerous schemes and tariffs - and so it's no surprise that it's something many individuals are starting to do.

Business owners benefit too. Consider a coffee shop, restaurant, or bar; they all rely on pulling in customers who are willing to buy. And the longer they can keep the customer on site, the more money they can make from them.

If this is something you are considering, think carefully before you sign on the dotted line. Recently, in the UK, a pub landlord was taken to court and fined a whopping £8000 simply because a customer in his pub used the Wi-Fi hotspot that the pub provided to download copyrighted material. This was believed to be the first case of its kind in the UK and the first time that a WI-FI hotspot provider has been held legally responsible for the activities of the users of the hotspot.

So be warned: If you make your hotspot available for others to use, you could end up in hot water. Even if you claim to not know what the users were doing (or downloading) you could end up footing a very expensive bill if it turns out they are downloading things that they shouldn't.

**What not to do:**

- Don't connect to Wi-Fi hotspots that do not have a password.

- Don't conduct financial transactions over a Wi-Fi hotspot.

- Don't forget to change default passwords on Wi-Fi networks that you set up.

- Don't forget to periodically review the settings on Wi-Fi networks that you set up.

# Lesson 7: Staying safe online

*"Everyone's online these days! FaceBook, Twitter, Myspace, LinkedIn, etc. How else can I tell what my old schoolmates are doing? Or see what my ex is having for lunch? And anyway, without Social Networks, how can I let everyone see the pics of my new car or show off about my upcoming holiday to Florida!?"*

There's no escaping it: Social Networks are here to stay. And even if they aren't, they aren't going anywhere anytime soon. And this is understandable - they're fun, interesting, and really useful for a multitude of things, including keeping in touch.

In fact, social networking is so pervasive that the smartphone and tablet manufacturers now sell their devices complete with social networking apps such as FaceBook already installed. However, they do have their downsides; some social networking apps will actually scan your address book and then send out an invitation to every contact. Many services will ask your permission before doing this, but some don't. So be aware of this.

Some manufacturers have even gone further than bundling apps with their devices – Apple's iOS 5 has social networking features built into the Operating System itself. For example if you tap a photo on an iOS 5 device, a menu appears with a list of things that you can do with that photo such as email it, send it via SMS or iMessage, print it, etc. but one of the more interesting options is *tweet*. Yes, Apple has integrated Twitter into the heart of iOS. No matter where you are when using your iPhone or iPad you have the option to tweet. But is that really a good thing?

## Oversharing

Yes and no. Obviously, social networking apps are great for some purposes, but some people tend to go overboard and end up oversharing their data. Oversharing is when your online accounts give away too much information to the bad guys. This leaves you wide open to Internet fraud and other forms of cybercrime: The 2010 State of the Net survey conducted by Consumer

Reports revealed that 52% of adult social network users left themselves open to potential cybercrime by oversharing their personal information.

I went to a family get-together at Christmas – we had a great time. The following day, a friend of mine called to say I looked like I was having fun on Christmas day! I asked how he knew. And said he saw it all on FaceBook.

But I've never had a FaceBook account in my life! Apparently, my son posted lots of Christmas day pictures on his FaceBook account. When I checked this, not only could I see all of his pictures, I could also see messages and other information that shouldn't have been public. Not only was he oversharing his information, he was oversharing mine too.

When using social networking services, it's important that you do not post personal information such as your date of birth, address, place of employment, or your hometown for others to see, especially on public profiles that anyone can view.

Showing your personal information on social networks can often give an identify thief key information about you needed to steal your identity. And remember once you've put it out there, that's it! You can't take it back no matter how much you try. Even if you close your account, your information has been posted, copied, backed-up, and replicated many times over and so you'll never be able to remove it entirely from the Internet.

## Gone Phishing…

The best way to catch a fish is to put a big, fat, juicy worm on a hook and dangle it right where the fish can see it. Sure enough, before you know it, you'll have a nibble or two, then a couple more, and finally a bite. And then you've got your fish; hook, line, and sinker.

Of course, this is a tried and tested technique that has worked for hundreds of thousands of years – so why shouldn't there be a cyber-equivalent?

The bad guys use the same tactic on you; Dangle some enticing bait, and then patiently sit back and wait for a bite. Phishing is generally performed via email – and so you can be duped on your smartphones or tablet in exactly the same way as you'll be duped on your desktop computer.

Phisihing emails generally appear to come from a legitimate organisation or company and will almost always contain links within the email requesting that you click the link to perform an action.

For example, I currently have an email in my inbox that appears to come from a well-known bank. The email proceeds to inform me that a large deposit has been made to my bank and that I need to log in to verify it. This sets alarm bells ringing for me for a couple of reasons:

- I don't have an account with said bank

- Even if I did have an account, why would I need to log in to verify a deposit?

The email then urges me to click a link to log in to my account. This sets further alarm bells ringing because the link doesn't appear to go to the bank's website.

On seeing this type of email, most users nowadays will delete it and move on to the next email. However, some don't. You see, the spammers who sent that email to 25,000 email addresses know that the vast majority of users won't even have an account at that bank, and that the vast majority of users will delete the email purely for that reason.

However, they also know that a certain percentage of users will have accounts at that bank. Further, they also know that some of those users will like the way that "money has been paid into your account" tends to flow off the lips quite nicely. And so finally, they know that a certain percentage of those users will click the link provided.

**So what happens when you click the link?**

Well – nothing spectacular. Your browser opens and you're whisked off to a website that looks surprisingly like the official bank's website. The logos are all present and correct. The fonts and typefaces used are correct, and the colours and layout of the site looks familiar.

However if you look closer, you'll see the colour of the logo is ever-so-slightly different. And you'll probably also notice that the text contains spelling errors or bad grammar.

Of course, you'll then be prompted to enter your credentials to log in, and when you do the bad guys will have got exactly what they want; your account details and password.

Obviously, this isn't the real bank's website so you won't be able to actually log in. So when you press ENTER, you'll very likely get an error saying that the website is currently down for maintenance and that you should try again later. Unfortunately, by the time you do get to log in at the official site, the bad guys will probably have beaten you to it.

Phishing emails have certain traits that make them easy to identify. You should be aware of these and always delete any suspicious emails without clicking on them:

- If a message doesn't greet you by name, it's very likely a phishing email.

- Messages with email addresses that don't come from the supposed sender.

- Messages that urge you to take action now!

- Messages with spelling or grammatical errors.

- Messages making offers that seem too good to be true.

## It's getting cloudy

Cloud computing is nothing new. Although the ideas behind it may have matured with age, the basic principle has been around a long time. But what exactly is cloud computing? And why has it suddenly come back into vogue again?

Essentially, cloud computing can be thought of as services being delivered to your computer over the Internet. Much like the way that electricity is delivered over the grid to your home or office, you don't need to know what goes on behind the scenes; you simply plug in, hook up, and go. You don't need to worry about updating programs or applying patches as everything is managed in the cloud by Amazon, Google, Apple, or whoever provides the cloud services to you.

These services can vary, but are typically productivity applications (word processing, spreadsheets, email) that help the user to get a job or task done.

One of its earliest proponents was Larry Ellison, the extravagant boss of Oracle. Back in the mid-nineties, Ellison proposed the Network Computer – a computer lacking any local storage that would connect to the Internet for storage and applications – as the next big thing.

Ellison reasoned that the lack of internal hardware would reduce the cost for consumers wanting to get on to the computing ladder. In addition, the lack of internal storage was marketed as a plus-point; customers' data would be stored on secure remote servers and would therefore be automatically backed-up regularly, freeing the user from this necessary chore. And Ellison's newly-formed company would benefit by providing the Network Computers themselves, as well as the Internet services needed to drive them.

Those services resembled the cloud services being made available today by companies such as Google, Apple and others. And of course the Network Computer would have been designed for web browsing.

Ellison's vision didn't quite take off, though; rapidly dropping PC prices meant that the cost of his Network Computers, with their reduced functionality, became a much less attractive option when compared to the only slightly more expensive 'proper' PCs that were flooding the market.

In addition, potential customers were put off by the idea of storing all of their data on remote servers; who would have access to all of this data? And exactly how secure was it?

With bigger and bigger question marks beginning to form, not surprisingly, the idea of consumers using a 'dumb' computer to access their networked data living in the cloud died a death.

However, lately, the idea has come back into favour – albeit in a different form to Ellison's original vision, which is probably why he has criticised the current rash of cloud computing announcements by major companies as being "complete gibberish" and "fashion driven". Whatever, mainly driven by the fast Internet connections that many people have and the experience gained in storing vast quantities of data by large corporations, cloud computing is here, and it looks like it's here to stay.

There are dangers, though. What happens when their systems are down? Do you then become unproductive? Will you be locked out of your account for days, or even weeks, on end? It makes sense, then, not to rely on a cloud computing vendor totally – always ensure that you have local copies of important documents or data that you can work on if you need to.

Also, once you've chosen a cloud computing provider, remember you'll gradually become 'locked-in' to their eco system, making it difficult to change to another provider when you want to.

But probably most importantly can you trust the company to store your information in the cloud securely? Are their systems robust enough to resist numerous attacks by cyber criminals?

Throughout 2011 there have been numerous high profile incidents where hackers had gained unauthorised access to user's data stored in the cloud.

**Case Study:** The Sony hack

On the 19th April 2011, Sony abruptly shut down its Sony Playstation gaming network when it discovered that hackers had gained access to the system. Sony had been the target of hackers on numerous occasions previously, so it came as no surprise to hear that their network had been attacked again. One week later, after extensive forensic examinations, the bombshell was dropped: the data of millions of users of Sony's Playstation Network (PSN) and its Qriocity music service had been compromised.

Initially, Sony reported that this amounted to 77 million user accounts, however this figure was later revised upwards to be in excess of 100 million. The group responsible, LulzSec even tweeted about the hack on Twitter:

*"1,000,000+ unencrypted users, unencrypted admin accounts, government and military passwords saved in plaintext. #PSN compromised. @Sony."*

The data collected about each user included usernames, passwords, credit card details, purchase histories and email addresses. Worse, and as per the tweet, much of this data was held in 'plain text' form. In other words, Sony was so confident of the security of their system that they didn't even bother to encrypt their users' data.

Because of the type of data that was compromised, it was clear that this was a major incident. The fact that the email addresses and passwords were recovered by the hackers in plain text meant that, in theory, those hackers also had access to other online accounts belonging to those users. Here's why: Because many of us have multiple online accounts - for example, for Amazon, eBay, email, Sony's PSN (ahem) – we tend to use the same password on each account, just to make things easier for us. I mean, no-one wants to remember 10 different passwords for 10 different online accounts, right?

The problem with this approach is, if someone finds out your password for one of those accounts, then they have your password for *all* of your accounts. So the intrusion into Sony's network was starting to look even worse then many had thought.

If you use the same password for multiple accounts, start changing them. Now. See *Lesson 10: Creating strong passwords* for ideas on creating strong passwords.

**Is it worth it?**

In this day and age, information is invaluable. Cyber criminals are out to get as much of your information as possible and storing this information online simply makes it easier for them to achieve their goals. Personally, I avoid social networking and cloud computing services, but this is becoming increasingly difficult to do - hence my joining the Twitter revolution recently. However the extent at which you put yourself, and your data, in the cloud is pretty much up to you.

**What not to do:**

- Don't reveal more information online than is absolutely necessary. Understand what you have posted about yourself on the various services.

- Don't put your phone number on social networking sites, or use it to enter online contests.

- Don't just accept friend requests blindly. Is the person really who they say they are? Or are they someone just out to pry into your affairs?

- Don't use the same password on multiple online accounts. If one account has been compromised, assume all accounts have been compromised and start changing passwords.

- Don't use Twitter's "tweet my location option". Unless you want to tell everyone your location every time you tweet.

- Don't share your location with everyone. If you use FaceBook Places, why not create a list with only your immediate family to share this information?

- Don't let other people share your location or check you in to places.

- Don't leave accounts open that you no longer use. If you don't use them, close them down.

# Lesson 8: Do I need an Anti-virus?

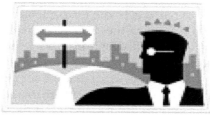

*"So what about computer viruses? I've had those on my PC in the past and they definitely aren't fun! Word viruses, stealth viruses, encrypted viruses… it's all so confusing. Can my phone get infected? Do I need an anti-virus program?"*

Well, in a word: No. Not for now, anyway.

To understand this, we first need to analyse and understand how viruses have become so entrenched on traditional computers. The desktop PC-based anti-virus industry is well established. I first became involved in 1993 when I started work with Alan Solomon on his ground breaking Anti-virus Toolkit.

Back then, in the early days, we only had to deal with a handful of viruses. And even then, the majority of them weren't really dangerous. We'd be fixing computers infected mainly with the Form boot sector virus, a couple of other partition sector infectors and a small number of file viruses. They were pretty easy to get a handle on initially and the majority of them were more of a nuisance than anything. However, as time went on, things started to ramp up and that handful of viruses that we were detecting soon exceeded 100!

When we were detecting over 500 viruses, I can remember colleagues saying "there's no way we'll get to 1000".

Now, in 2012, there are hundreds of thousands of viruses on the loose – a staggering amount. So surely your smartphone is vulnerable, then?

Actually, this isn't the case. Even though viruses are an everyday fact of life for traditional PCs the good news is that things are not so established on the mobile front; the virus threat is very much in its infancy again on mobile platforms and there are some important usage and design differences that will help to ensure that viruses on mobile phones will remain few and far between.

### But what exactly is a virus?

A virus is a computer program (or a 'piece of code') that is capable of replicating (i.e. making copies of itself) and spreading. Back in the day, people used to write viruses for fun and pleasure. Similar to graffiti, it was a counter-culture way of showing how skilled you were at programming. Now, however, viruses are written and used by the bad guys to steal money from unsuspecting users.

When a computer virus is run, it gets into the computer's Random Access Memory (also known as RAM) and tries to infect other things. One of the traditional ways that a computer virus spreads is via removable media such as disks or memory sticks. For example, the virus would get into RAM and, when a disk or memory stick was inserted into the computer, the virus would stealthily write a copy of itself to the media. Alternatively, the virus would look for executable programs on the disk and infect those. You wouldn't notice this happening, of course, and so when you inserted the memory stick or disk into another computer and ran programs from it, the virus would infect the new computer too.

### The Perfect Storm

Traditional computer viruses were able to spread and become entrenched for a number of reasons:

### Numbers

The sheer popularity of Microsoft's Disk Operating System (DOS) and, later, Windows 3.x meant that viruses had large numbers of potential computers to infect. DOS and Windows were by far the most dominant platforms in the '90s - much more dominant than the Mac at the time which is one of the reasons why the Mac was a much less enticing proposition for virus writers; why waste your time writing a virus for a system with less than 5% market share, when it was easier to write for the other 95%?

### Technology and behaviours

Computers of the day were very reliant on external media such as floppy disks to function. Many programs such as word processors or spreadsheets came loaded on floppy disks (and typically multiple floppy disks) and in lots of cases these disks would need to be left in the floppy disk drive for the program to work. In addition, many computers needed to 'boot up' from a floppy disk in order to load the operating system so that the user could get to work. Thus floppy disks (whether the old 5 inch variant or the newer 3.5 inch type) became a target for viruses.

Floppy disks were swapped between computers and shared between users which resulted in a perfect environment for viruses to quickly spread; an infected floppy disk left in the drive while the computer booted up would invariably result in the computer becoming infected.

## Ignorance

Way back then, computer viruses were new. Many people had not even heard of them, and those that did had no idea of what they were or how they worked. Because of these factors, viruses had an easy time spreading from computer to computer. Many users would mistake any symptoms of infection for bugs or hardware problems; for example users whose computers were infected with the Form virus would think they had a hardware problem with their keyboard as the virus would make the keys beep if they were pressed on a particular day of the month. The fact that they had a virus wouldn't cross their minds and so their disk swapping and sharing behaviours would continue unabated.

## Lack of security

The early DOS and Windows operating systems were simply not very secure. They weren't designed for the threats that were starting to become apparent and were not 'hardened' enough to repel the viruses that were starting to become prevalent, which is why anti-virus programs became (and still are) an important part of computer security; once viruses were able to get a 'foothold' it would prove impossible to eradicate them.

Operating systems such as Unix and Linux have security inherently built into their core, which is why viruses are rarely seen on these platforms. The DOS and Windows platforms eschewed the complexity of security meaning that their relative simplicity and accessibility, while good for end-users, left them wide open to debilitating virus infections.

Now that you have a clear idea of how computer viruses gained a foothold in the PC environment, let's make the cases for and against viruses spreading in the same way on mobile devices.

## The case for running anti-virus

## The numbers

Smartphone usage is exploding and, as we've said before, criminals follow crowds. The sheer number of current smartphone users coupled with the explosive growth in smartphone and tablet sales projected for the next couple of years makes smartphones a prime target for the bad guys.

A recent report by market research firm Gartner predicts massive growth in the smartphone market for 2012 and 2013 with Android-powered devices leading the way. In fact, Gartner predicts that worldwide smartphone sales will top 470 million units by the end of 2011, with Android devices making up 38% of these. By the end of 2012, Gartner expects this figure to reach 50%. All of this is good news for the bad guys as they can see a massive market opportunity.

## The users

Just like in the early days of viruses on traditional computers, the average smartphone user has no real idea of the potential threats that they face, or that are even possible. On traditional computers, malware and viruses still find it easy to infect a host because the user *allows* them to. For example, malware typically infects a computer when the user visits a compromised website in their web browser. Typically, a message will pop up telling the user that problems have been detected on their computer and that they can fix the problems by downloading a program that the website recommends.

At this point the user's computer is actually *clean* and free from viruses or malware, however the message fools the user into thinking otherwise.

The program that the message advises on downloading is a Trojan. Crucially, if the user downloads and installs the program to their computer, the Trojan will run and compromise the user's computer. The computer is referred to as compromised because at this point the Trojan can download and install other programs, Trojans, viruses or malware by itself with no user involvement. These programs can then allow the bad guys to gain access to the compromised computer, allowing them to copy and read documents, etc.

This is a tried and tested mechanism that the bad guys use in order to get their Trojans and malware onto the computer of an unsuspecting user. The willingness of users to say 'yes' to prompts where they should really say 'no' is what the bad guys rely on to successfully gain access to the computer.

The propensity of users towards saying 'yes' on their PCs and providing access to things when they shouldn't do, translates worryingly well to smartphones where users allow apps access to things that they shouldn't have access to. For example why does a note-taking app with no location-related features want permissions to access your location as well as your contacts? When prompted, many users blindly click 'allow' without a second's notice or hesitation, resulting in them losing control of their device.

Identity thieves have established this vector as one of the most common ways that they will gain access to a user's private and personal information.

## Social Networking

In the traditional PC world, viruses have been seen to spread via social networking channels very quickly. This is because, by their very nature, social networks allow people to share. This inevitably leads to users sharing links to compromised websites which will attempt to install malware and viruses onto computers that visit those sites. In addition, social networks experience a high degree of phishing and social engineering (where an individual attempts to trick someone into running programs, accessing websites, or divulging information that they shouldn't).

## The case against running anti-virus

## Robust OS

Computer viruses found it easy to gain a foothold on the traditional PC market because the Operating Systems of the day, such as DOS and Windows, were not very secure. DOS was designed to be flexible and easy to use from the 'command line' but it had no defences against viruses. While Windows 3.x (which ran 'on top' of DOS) was a little more secure, the limitations and weaknesses of DOS still made the whole ensemble vulnerable to viruses and other nasties.

Since those days, the architects and developers of Operating Systems have put security at the heart of their offerings; in this day and age an Operating System that does not take security seriously is an Operating System that will die a death very quickly.

In practice, this means that modern Operating Systems such as Google's Android, Microsoft's Windows Phone 7, RIM's Blackberry OS, Apple's iOS, and others are all super-secure.

Indeed Android has a Linux-based kernel which is a good, secure place to start building an OS. Similarly, iOS is derived from Apple's desktop Mac OS X with which it shares common Unix foundations – again making it inherently secure.

## The Sandbox

Another security technique employed by modern Operating Systems is the sandbox. As its name implies a sandbox is a secure designated virtual area that an app can play in to its hearts content. While the app can run happily in this area, the sandbox severely limits what the app has access to. For example the sandbox ensures that the app does not have access to your browsing history, contacts, or your Bluetooth or Wi-Fi, unless you explicitly grant it access to these things.

To keep your device secure, the rule of thumb that you should abide to is to keep as much of the app in its sandbox as possible. In practice, this means not allowing or not granting permissions to an app when the permission requests are made during the installing the app.

PC based operating systems didn't attempt to sandbox applications in the same way, meaning that a program running on a PC would have far reaching and unhindered access to every part of the system. As sandboxes are now integral to most smartphone OSes, apps will generally only be allowed to gain access to your personal and private information if you let them play outside the sandbox by granting them permissions that they do not require.

## Infection mechanisms

As previously mentioned, viruses would spread from PC to PC because users frequently swapped infected floppy discs, memory sticks and other types of media. This method of infection does not lend itself to smartphones and tablets for obvious reasons – they do not employ disks or CDs. Some smartphones and tablets do utilise memory cards, but these are not swapped between devices and users to the extent that disks used to be and, anyway, the memory cards are not used to 'boot up' these devices.

## Battery life/Performance may be affected

When running an anti-virus program on your computer, there has always been a trade-off between performance and security; the more securely your anti-virus was configured, the slower the computer would run. The less securely the anti-virus was configured, the faster the computer would work.

This is because anti-virus programs add an 'overhead'. The computer has to work harder while the anti-virus performs its checks. When using a word processing app, this slowdown in performance is barely perceptible. However, on something a little more demanding such as a game, the drop in performance becomes noticeable as the game begins to respond slowly or become 'laggy'. This is caused by a couple of reasons: any anti-virus program running on the device will take up processor time from other apps such as the game, but also the anti-virus will take up crucial memory on your device, restricting the memory that is available for other apps.

In addition, with the processor working harder more power is drawn from the battery which results in shorter average battery life.

These compromises in battery life and performance make it unattractive to run an anti-virus program on a smartphone.

## No real viruses

Let's get this straight – viruses and malware are different things. Malware doesn't self-replicate in the same way that viruses do. Malware is a program that you have to explicitly install and run which then does something bad, whereas viruses have the ability to spread from computer to computer by themselves, install themselves, and then do something bad. But as of December 2011 (when this eBook was written) there have been no real viruses produced for the popular smartphone platforms. So if there are no real viruses, why do you need an anti-virus?

Yes – I do know that there have been viruses developed for some of the older smartphone platforms but, to all intents and purposes, those old platforms are pretty much irrelevant now; Android, iOS, Windows Phone 7 and RIM are the platforms of note – and there are currently no real virus threats on these platforms.

## The verdict

Taking all of the above into account, the use of an anti-virus program on a smartphone is not recommended at this time. Of course things may change, and if they do I'll produce a second revision of this book.

The fact that there are no real smartphone viruses around to infect the major smartphone platforms, together with the increased security of these platforms means that, for now at least, it's simply not necessary or desirable.

Why reduce the performance of your device searching for viruses that do not exist?

Also, don't be tempted by free anti-virus apps. Remember the saying "you pays your money and makes your choice". Well, you didn't actually pay any money, did you? That speaks volumes. You'll be installing an app that won't find any threats on your device, but will bug you with adverts every time it's run.

## So what about anti-malware software?

This is one area where I believe we'll see movement on smartphone devices. While viruses in the classical sense don't really exist for smartphones, Trojans most certainly do. So maybe the anti-virus companies need to start developing anti-malware software instead. This would make *much* more sense.

## What not to do:

- Don't run an antivirus program on your smartphone. You'll suffer a loss in performance and battery life for no gain.

- Don't confuse viruses with malware or trojans. Viruses spread by themselves whereas malware has to be installed and run manually on a smartphone or computer. While malware is a major problem on smartphones, viruses are not.

- Don't install apps without checking how safe they are. As mentioned before, always install apps from a known, secure source – don't just download them from any dodgy-looking website.

- Don't side-load apps. In other words, only install your apps from official app stores.

- Don't always 'allow' requests for permissions. If you don't think an app should have access to your contacts, disallow it.

# Lesson 9: Jailbreaking

*"I've been wanted to jailbreak my phone for a while. A friend of mine jailbroke his iPhone and now doesn't need to pay for any apps. How cool is that. There can't be any downsides to that, can there?"*

While the vast majority of smartphone users are happy with the way their devices work, there are some more adventurous souls who like to try and get that little bit extra. For those users, jailbreaking, or rooting, has become an attractive option.

Jailbreaking is an act performed on Apple iOS devices, whereas rooting is typically performed on Android devices. The effect of either is the same: the device is 'opened up' which means it can now run apps and do things that it was not able to do prior to being jailbroken or rooted. Importantly, however, jailbreaking or rooting a device can result in the removal of security mechanisms that are put in place to keep the device secure. This is why, for some people, jailbreaking or rooting can be a risky procedure.

## Jailbreaking 101

Because jailbreaking and rooting essentially mean the same thing, I'll collectively refer to the act as jailbreaking, unless I'm specifically talking about rooting on an Android device.

When Apple rolled out the iPhone in 2007, complaints started arising from a small percentage of users that the 'closed model' Apple had employed for customizing and running apps on the device was too restrictive. In other words, users didn't like the fact that Apple restricted the apps that could be run on the device to the small number of apps that came with the phone by default, even when it was clear that the iPhone was capable of doing much more.

Apple, and to be more precise Steve Jobs, wanted to have full control over the iPhone experience and 'locking down' the apps that could be run on the device was one way of doing this. Developers eager to show what they, and the iPhone, could do were soon discovering ways of writing apps and getting them to run on the iPhone through the 'back door'. And so jailbreaking was born.

But it wasn't just about the apps; By jailbreaking a device, users were able to change the look of the app icons, the wallpaper (this was before iOS allowed you to change the wallpaper) and extensively personalize the device by adding different themes and fonts; again, the iPhone was very capable of handling this type of customization, but at the time Apple made a business decision to restrict users from this type of activity.

After time, Apple relented and launched the iPhone developer program and App store which provided developers with a legitimate way of writing apps for the iPhone and distributing them to users. The catch was that the new App store was the only legitimate way to get apps onto the iPhone, and developers had to stick to strict guidelines when submitting an app to the store; if their app flaunted any of the rules, it would be rejected and not allowed on the store.

By jailbreaking their devices, users were also able to do other things like sync their content via Wi-Fi and enable their iPhones to be used as Wi-Fi hotspots. In addition, developers were able to create apps that performed functions that would not be allowed if the developer tried to submit his app through the rigid App store approval process.

Another popular reason for jailbreaking is to allow a device such as an iPhone to run on a different carrier or network to the one it is locked to.

Lastly, many people (not all) jailbreak their devices in order to gain access to free apps that they would normally have to pay for – this is because the apps are 'cracked', and is the only problem that I personally have with jailbreaking; if you want to enable features that were previously restricted or blocked, then jailbreaking is an option. However, if you only want to jailbreak in order to not pay for apps that developers have put a lot of hard work into, then that's not very cool.

Many of the features that users would jailbreak for have been incorporated into subsequent versions of iOS which shows that Apple is, at least, listening to customer's requests. Similarly, Android users can root their devices to enable new functionality, however rooting on Andorid devices is not as liberating as jailbreaking an iOS device. This is because iOS devices are much more tightly controlled than Andoid devices – for example, with iOS you can normally only get apps from the Apple app store unless you jailbreak. However, with Android you are able to get apps from the Android market as well as sideload apps from other sources even before you root the device.

On Android devices, one of the other benefits of rooting is that you'll be able to overclock the device. This means you can make the processor run at a higher number of 'clock cycles' (in other words, faster) than what the manufacture specified. This means that programs that you run on the device will run faster than before. While this obviously sounds appealing, be aware that after overclocking in this way your battery life will be dramatically shortened. What? You didn't think the manufacturer would slow down the processor for no good reason, did you?

### But who creates the Jailbreak, and how?

The first thing to understand is that the individuals or groups who create a jailbreak, are not bad guys or criminals; they're pretty clever computer programmers who simply want to make their smartphone or tablet do things that, for whatever reason, they're restricted from doing. Essentially, the jailbreaker removes the restrictions that Apple, Google, or Microsoft put on their devices.

In fact, jailbreaking is becoming so mainstream that the jailbreaking community have regular conferences where they can meet up, share information, and learn new techniques.

Problems come into play if the user carrying out the jailbreak doesn't fully understand what they're doing, or how to best configure their device after the Jailbreak.

As mentioned, many people Jailbreak in order to 'open up' their device. But what many people don't realise is that they haven't just opened up their device; they've opened up their device to being hacked.

This is because they neglected to change the default 'root' password after jailbreaking – and if someone has your root password, and your phone has been stripped of its normal defence mechanisms (as it's been jailbroken), they can access your device and pretty much do whatever they want with it.

The bad guys are able to tell what weakness your device has (such as a default root password) by running code that looks for exploits – essentially, back doors that allows someone to gain access without you realising.

A while back, a Dutch hacker set out to show users of jailbroken iPhones how unsecure their phones were by running a 'port scanning' utility that would identify any jailbroken phones that still had the default password in place. When it found such a phone, it would send a message to the phone that read "Your iPhone's been hacked because it's really insecure! Please visit <*website*> and secure your iPhone right now! Right now, I can access all your files. This message won't disappear until your iPhone's secure."

When the user clicked on the link in the message, it took them to Paypal where they would be asked to pay €5 in order to remove the hack. However, after a backlash from users and the media, the hacker relented and started providing users with details onhow to remove the hack manually. In addition, after a major change of heart, the hacker also decided to return the money that users had already paid him.

So it goes without saying: if you do jailbreak your iPhone, don't leave the default root password in place. Make sure this is changed immediately as the default root password for all iPhones is well known – a quick search on Google will tell you what it is – and so it's inherently unsafe.

As mentioned previously, the guys who actually develop the jailbreaks are not bad guys. In fact, the skills of these programmers hasn't gone unnoticed; FaceBook has employed a former jailbreaker known as GeoHot after his jailbreaking of Apple iOS devices and even Sony's PS3 impressed them, and another former jailbreaker known as Comex has actually found employment at Apple after they saw his programming skills.

In order to create a jailbreak for a device, the programmers search the operating system and its associated applications for bugs and errors that they can exploit. Bugs that cause an app to crash become candidates and are studied closely to see if they can be used to form an entry-point for a jailbreak.

Apple actually uses the fact that the programmers have to crash apps multiple times against them: with every crash that occurs on an iOS smartphone or tablet, a crash report is generated. Then, whenever the device is synced with iTunes, the crash report is sent to Apple. Apple analyses these in order to help it identify and fix problems, but this also means that they can identify crashes that the jailbreakers are trying to exploit. This way, Apple can fix the issue and close up the loophole in the form of a software update delivered before or just after the jailbreaker releases their next jailbreak.

This isn't the end of the story, though; a cat and mouse game is developing as the jailbreakers have produced a utility to capture these crash reports and redirect them to the jailbreakers, thus bypassing Apple altogether. The fact that many thousands of users have downloaded and are actively using the utility shows that jailbreaking is, and will remain for some time, an extremely popular way

**Bricking**

Invariably, when jailbreaking or rooting a device there will be times when things go wrong. And if things go wrong during the jailbreaking process you can very easily end up with what's known technically as a 'bricked' phone. In other words, your super-cool phone that was previously able to surf the web, pick up email, play videos, etc. can no longer do any of that. In fact, it can't even turn on any more. And so, essentially, it's as useful as useful as a housebrick. You can pick it up, bang it, shake it, plug things into it all to no avail; your phone has now turned into a really cool-looking paperweight.

This has happened to me in the past when jailbreaking was fairly new. The newer jailbreaks are much more robust and less likely to brick your device, but it can (and does) still happen. Therefore if your technical skills are not as good as you would like them to be, you might want to avoid the temptation to jailbreak.

## It started with the iPod

Jailbreaking and 'modding' devices is nothing new. Whenever there's a cool device that appears to be limited in some way, human nature compels some individuals to try to plug that gap – to try to modify that device to make it do things that it can't do in its natural form.

I purchased my first iPod (a third generation model) back in 2003. Six months or so later I modded it to install and run Linux! Back then, iPods were nothing like what they are now. This was way before the iPod was able to show pictures and play video, receive email, surf the Internet, etc. In fact, the OS was pretty darn basic; it played music – and that was it!

Sometime in early 2004, I heard stories about a group of individuals who had managed to install Linux onto their iPods, enabling them to do all manner of funky stuff – including playing Doom. Yes, *Doom*! After hearing that, I just had to get Linux installed on my iPod too. And so, lo and behold: shortly thereafter my 3rd generation, touch wheel iPod was running *iPodLinux*.

iPodLinux took the place of the normal OS whenever the iPod was 'booted' up. It provided the user with a new User Interface and, amongst other things, allowed them to play games that were not available on those early iPods. However, to my dismay, I was never able to get Doom to work.

All other features worked as expected though, and I found great joy in showing my other techie buddies how I had Linux running on my iPod. However, the sheen quickly wore off. Overall, I found the new User Interface to be slow and clunky; even though it was very similar to Apple's standard OS, it lacked the finesse that I had become used to.

The novelty of seeing the iPodLinux penguin logo also wore off after a month or so, and so a short time later, I decided to revert back to the standard OS.

## Interest piqued

After seeing Linux running on the iPod, I decided to experiment with other ways of increasing the functionality of the device. I tinkered and played and found some interesting things. One of these was the Notes feature of iPod OS. Now, to most people, the Notes feature would not be anything special – but to me, it was a thing of beauty. (Yes – I'm definitely a nerd).

You see, it was extremely structured and all XML-based. This meant that as long as you formatted your content correctly, you could upload all sorts of data to the iPod and have it displayed through the Notes feature. As long as it was text, of course. I really didn't know what to do with it all, though – and so after a while I got involved in other projects.

Then, in 2005 I took a trip from London to New York with my wife. Being tech-savvy, before we left, I used a number of websites to plan our itinerary and work out the best places to go and best things to do. I downloaded the relevant pages, put them all together and printed them out. But in our hurry to get to the airport, I managed to leave all of my printouts on the dining-room table. DOH!.

One trans-Atlantic flight later, a business idea was born.

As I was listening to Ray Charles through my white buds, I contemplated how for many people iPods had become an essential travel accessory. At around the same time I remembered the Notes feature that I had been tinkering with months ago. Why not load the travel data into Notes and view it on your iPod?

Throughout the entire time I was in New York, I mulled over how I could implement the idea. By the time I got back to the UK I had a good handle on what I wanted to do, and so I started developing a website. In the summer of 2006, I launched expodition.com. Expodition provided users of Apple's iPod with a location-based service - allowing them to type in a postcode (zip code) of the area they were travelling to, in order to receive a 'snapshot' of that area in a format that could be viewed through the iPod's Notes feature. To power the site, I did a deal with upmystreet.com whom I sourced the information from.

These snapshots were personalized and tailored to each user based on the user's profile, which specified tastes such as favourite types of food, whether the user liked pubs, clubs, museums, etc.

At the time, the service provided by Expodition was ground-breaking - mainly because it gave iPods a new purpose for travelling users. Now, in addition to getting music and video from their iPods, users were also able to get detailed information about their intended destination.

Little did I know that just six months later – in January 2007 – Apple would announce the iPhone. And the Internet-enabled iPhone, together with the iPod touch, killed that website dead.

But I digress.

The point of my rambling is to point out that individuals will always attempt to expand on the features built into any device, pushing that device to its very limits. So jailbreaking or modding is, and will continue to be, an inevitable consequence of the smartphone or tablet scene.

## Violations

If you are using your jailbroken or rooted device as a personal hotspot or for tethering purposes, be aware that you may be breaking your service provider's terms and conditions of service. This could result in you being cut off and, depending on how serious your abuse is, legal action being taken against you. In reality the legal action probably won't happen, but your service provider reserves its right to do this.

Google and Microsoft take a relaxed view on rooting or jailbreaking their devices. Apple, however, have remained defiant in their view that their iOS devices should not be jailbroken and, for anyone who does, their warranties are voided. Consequently, with each new version of iOS, Apple makes it increasingly harder to jailbreak.

Jailbreaking of iOS devices is legal in the United States courtesy of a July 2010 ruling by the Library of Congress which said it was permissible to circumvent access controls to a copyrighted operating system as long as the aim was to install lawfully obtained software – in other words you're not allowed to install apps that have been hacked to make them free.

Jailbreaking is also legal in the UK – but be aware that you'll void your warranty in the process. This means that if your device develops a fault and you bring it to Apple hoping for help or a replacement, as soon as they see it's been jailbroken they will very likely tell you that you're out of luck.

## What not to do:

- Don't jailbreak or root your device without fully understanding the process and the consequences.

- Don't leave the default root passwords in place. Change them as soon as you've jailbroken your device.

- Don't confuse the guys who produce the jailbreaks with the bad guys. They are not one in the same.

- Don't jailbreak just to get cracked or free software. That's not a cool thing to do.

# Lesson 10: Creating your password

*"I have passwords for this, passwords for that, passwords for so many different things! It's crazy - which is why I generally use the same password for everything. It means I'll never get locked out because I'll never forget my password!"*

As we've mentioned before in this book, there's one really important thing standing between your private or sensitive data, and the hackers; your password.

In this final lesson, we'll cover some of the points that will help you create strong, secure passwords that are easy for you to remember, but difficult for others to crack.

Passwords are a thorny subject. They are essential for the security of our smartphones and computers, as they allow us to authenticate ourselves. In other words, they help us to prove that we are who we say we are and thus allow us to log into different online services securely. In this day and age, they're essential.

However they need to be chosen with care. Many people tend to put little thought into this aspect of smartphone or tablet security, resulting in them settling for passwords that are weak, commonly used, and easily guessed.

So first, a bit of trivia: In a 2011 report compiled by Splashdata, the top 10 most commonly used passwords were:

- password
- 123456
- 12345678
- qwerty
- abc123

- monkey
- 1234567
- letmein
- trustno1
- dragon

Yes, believe it or not many people still use the word 'password' as a password. Not only that, but it's probably the most commonly used password around the world as well!

It doesn't take a genius, then, to realise that if you are using any of these as a password to your smartphone or tablet you might as well have no password set at all. People use the passwords above because they're easy to remember: "What's my password? Oh yes – 'password'". But unfortunately, this also means that they're also easy for others to guess.

What these people fail to realise is that you can have easy-to-remember passwords which are also difficult for others to guess. So if you are using an easily-guessed password, you need to get it changed straight away.

### Same password, multiple accounts

Remember the Sony hack that we discussed previously? The major problem there was that the hackers managed to get their hands on a full complement of data for each customer account – including the individual email addresses and passwords. This is a problem because, as many people use the same email address/password combination on a number of different websites, the hackers were then conceivably able to gain access to those sites; By gaining access to the password and email combination for each user for the Sony site, the hackers were also able to use this combination to log in to many other sites.

For example, high profile sites that many users have access to and which require an email address and password to log in (such as FaceBook, eBay, or Amazon) would be the first targets.

The most obvious lesson here, then, is: Don't use the same email and password combination to log into different sites. Instead, why not create a number of different email addresses? (it's not against the law) and use these to log into the different services. You'll only need two or three, but even if you used the same password with those (which I don't recommend you do) it would make it much more difficult for someone to access your other services if they obtained one of your email/password combinations.

So think how much more difficult it would be if you used different passwords for each account, too?

So with multiple passwords, how do you make them easy to remember? Use this technique to create easy-to-remember, hard-to-crack passwords that can be applied to different websites.

- First, what site are you creating the password for? In this example, let's choose eBay.

- Next, think of a phrase that you can associate with this site. For example:

  I love to sell my old schmutter on eBay

  Rods Tip: A phrase that you associate with the site will make it easy to remember every time you start logging on.

- Next, take the first letter of each word, like so: Iltsmosoe

- Add some numbers into the mix – for example, change the I to a 1, and change the t to a 2 and maybe change the last o to a zero: 1l2smos0e

Of course, if you're feeling adventurous, you could make it even stronger by adding upper-case letters and symbols.

Get the idea? Now that's a strong password that would be pretty difficult to crack but would be easy for you to remember.

That was eBay. Maybe your password for FaceBook would be: **K1twf&fi$0F**

*Keeping in touch with friends and family in Spain on FaceBook*

**I forgot**

Many hackers will also get into your account by using the 'I forgot' or 'reset my password' link. We've all used this type of recovery method to get into an account from time to time. However it's important to realise that some systems are more secure than others. For example, systems that use a pre-set series of questions are not the most secure because the set of questions for the hacker to answer are quite narrow.

When setting up a new account, if you are asked for a set of recovery questions try not to use information that is easy to find out about you such as your high school; if you've plastered your school all over FaceBook or Friends Reunited, then it's going to be pretty easy for someone with a good search engine to successfully reset your password.

Remember these additional points:

- As mentioned above, don't use the same password for all of your sites and services. If you do, and someone gets hold of your password, they then have the passwords to all of your sites.

- Don't use common or 'normal' words – even written backwards. They can easily be revealed by various methods that hackers use, including a type called a 'dictionary attack'. Essentially, avoid 'real' words that can be found in dictionaries.

- Don't use sequences or repeated characters in passwords. For example, 123456, 111111, or abcdef.

- Don't use your pet's name, your name, or any other names for that matter. Names are always revealed on social networking websites which makes it easier for hackers to gain access.

- In fact, don't use any personally identifiable information.

- Don't use the same password for ever! It's good to change your password on a regular basis.

- Don't use default passwords. Many websites or services will assign your account with a default password when you create an account. Remember to go into 'Settings' or 'Account Management' and change this the first time you log into your account.

- Don't write your password down!

- Make your password at least 8 characters long. The longer your password, the more difficult it is to uncover it. For example, if your password was abc there are only 6 possible password combinations to find! Not very hard. However, if you add some numbers into the mix, for example: abc123, there are now close to 1000 different combinations! The more characters you add, the combinations grow exponentially. By adding just one more: abc1234, there are now 6000 different combinations.

## Pattern swiping

Some Android devices allow you to use a relatively new method of authenticating known as 'pattern swiping' in order to set an unlock 'code'. This is typically a grid of nine dots which you join together by swiping your finger through a pre-determined route, joining the dots as you go. This is quite an intuitive way of securing your device as it's much harder for someone to guess your swipe. For example, where does it start from? And how many dots are linked? Not everyone gets on with pattern swiping, but it's worth a try just to see if it will work for you.

## Facial recognition

This is another promising way of ensuring that the device is only unlocked by the registered owner. With facial recognition systems, first introduced to tablets and smartphones with Google's Android OS, the user simply brings the device up to their face and waits for the device to recognize them in order to gain access. This method means that the user does not need to supply a password, PIN, or swipe a pattern in order to start using the device.

There are some pitfalls, though; the technology is very new and is nowhere near as reliable as a strong password. It's possible that the system might lock users out if it doesn't recognise them properly, (maybe due to lighting conditions, etc.) or allow someone who has similar features to gain access inadvertently.

It has even been possible to compromise facial recognition systems with the use of a picture of the registered user! Therefore, at this point, I wouldn't recommend using facial recognition as a way of securing your smartphone or tablet. As with most things, though, the technology will improve with time.

## Automatic Wipe

Some devices can be configured to automatically wipe all data if an incorrect password has been entered a certain number of times. For example, if an incorrect password has been tried ten times in a row it's likely that the phone is not in the possession of its rightful owner, and so all content can safely be deleted.

Remember you backed-up your device before you set off on your vacation, right? So really, it doesn't matter if the phone is wiped; if you find it again, or when you get a replacement, you can sync your data back on.

# Good Luck!

I wrote this eBook with the intention that it would empower you to use your smartphone or tablet safely, thus minimising the potential of you being hacked or being made a victim of identity theft through your new device; By sticking to the advice given in the various lessons, you'll thwart the hackers at every turn.

You've learned why identity thieves want your information, what they can do with it, and the techniques they use to get hold of it.

You've learned how to use Wi-Fi networks securely and how to identify suspect networks before you connect to them.

Now, you'll realise why apps attempt to determine your location when they have no business in doing so, and you've seen that in the vast majority of cases, it's OK to restrict what these apps have access to.

You've learned why the manufacturers are storing your data in the cloud and the steps that they are (hopefully) taking to secure that data. And the list goes on.

Hopefully, this eBook has given you the ammunition you need to start using your smartphone or tablet with confidence.

Before I sign off, here are two last tips that can help you avoid becoming a victim:

- Don't let anyone install programs onto your smartphone without seeing exactly what they are doing or what they are installing. Just recently I saw someone at my local gym do this and was surprised that they were given access so easily.

- Don't sell or give your phone away without performing a factory reset – essentially wiping your phone and restoring it to the state it was in when you bought it.

So now that you've been armed, it's up to you to.

Good Luck!

Rod.

# Glossary

Use this glossary to help you to understand some of the security-related terms used in this book. Some of the terms listed in the glossary are not mentioned in the book, but are included here for your reference.

**Access Control**

A means of ensuring that only specified users are granted access to specific resources, such as a database.

**Account Harvesting**

A means of gathering account names and data from a computer system.

**Active Content**

This typically refers to 'code' that has been placed in a web page or web app. That code is run on your computer or smartphone when the page is opened by a web browser on the device. Active content is mainly safe and does things like animate pictures or adverts on the page. However some active content can be bad and do undesirable things to your computer, smartphone, or tablet.

**Algorithm**

A specific set of step-by-step instructions that can be followed to solve a problem, often mathematical. Algorithms are normally implemented by a computer but can also be followed by a human.

**App**

A program that runs on a smartphone or tablet computer.

**Authentication**

Authentication is the process of confirming that a person is actually who they say they are. For example, when you pay for an item with your credit card, you authenticate yourself by typing in your PIN.

**Authorization**

When someone has been given approval or permission to do something, (for example to view account details in a database) this is known as authorization.

**Backdoor**

Like its name implies, when a hacker installs a backdoor onto your computer or smartphone, it allows them to access your device whenever they want. A backdoor is typically installed after the system has been compromised by malware.

## Biometrics

Biometrics use the physical characteristics of a user (such as fingerprints or a retina scan) to determine whether the user has access to a device or resource. This type of authentication will become more commonplace in smartphones and tablets.

## Brute Force

A technique of gaining access to a device or resource through the exhaustive, repetitive testing of all possibilities - for example, working through every word and combination of words in a dictionary - attempting to find a password. Brute force attacks are crude and require a lot of time to implement.

## Buffer Overflow

A buffer overflow occurs when a program or process tries to store more data in a buffer (temporary data storage area) than the buffer was designed to hold. The extra data cannot fit into the buffer and so overflows into other areas of memory. This overflow can cause problems by overwriting valid data. When a hacker instigates a buffer overflow, he can craft it so that it places code into memory that can be executed.

## Checksum

A checksum is used to detect changes in an object. In most cases, the checksum is derived from the item itself. For example, a checksum of a document may be obtained by running a specific algorithm against that document. Whenever that algorithm is used again on the document, the checksum should always be the same. If the checksum is different, the contents of the document have changed.

## Cipher

An algorithm that is used for encrypting and decrypting data.

## Ciphertext

Encrypted messages are sent from one location to another in ciphertext.

## Compromise

If your computer, smartphone, or website has been hacked without your knowledge, the hacker can lessen the security or leave 'holes' open in order to easily gain access in the future. Your computer, smartphone, or website is then said to be compromised.

## Computer Network

A collection of computers connected together either physically (via cable) or virtually (for example, via Wi-FI) to enable them to exchange files and data.

## Cookie

Websites accessed through a web browser typically use cookies to store information about their state on the computer or smartphone accessing the site. This information can be retained even when the computer is no longer connected to the website. Passwords can be stored in cookies so that when you visit the website again it 'remembers' your passwords and other settings so that you don't need to type them again.

## Data Aggregation

Data Aggregation is a method of analyzing several different, but related, records with the goal of building a 'bigger picture' of the data as a whole.

## Day Zero

Day Zero (or Zero Day) is the day a new vulnerability is made known. In some cases, a zero day exploit is referred to as an exploit for which no patch currently available.

## Decryption

Decryption is the process of transforming an encrypted message back into its original plaintext form.

## Demilitarized Zone (DMZ)

A demilitarized zone (DMZ) is a network area that sits between an organization's internal, secured network (sometimes called an Intranet) and an external, unsecured network, usually the Internet.

## Denial of Service (DoS) attack

An attack aimed at disrupting the service provided by, for example, a website. An attacker may use various techniques to overload the website or service it provides in order to prevent legitimate users from accessing the service.

## Dictionary Attack

An attack that attempts to discover a password by trying all of the phrases or words contained in a 'dictionary' or list. Dictionary attacks uses predefined list of words. This is different to a brute force attack which attempts to discover the password by trying all possible combinations.

## Digital Certificate

A digital certificate is an electronic certificate or passport issued by a certificate authority that establishes your credentials when doing business or other transactions over the Internet.

## Digital Signature

A digital signature is a hash of a message that can uniquely identify the sender of the message. The digital signature can also prove that the message hasn't been changed during transmission.

## Encryption

The transformation of plaintext data into a form known as cipher text. Encryption is a method used to hide the original content.

## Firewall

A logical or physical barrier in a network which prevents unauthorized access to data or resources. For example, a firewall can stop hackers on the Internet accessing the data on your device or smartphone.

## Flooding

An attack that attempts to cause a failure in a computer system by providing more input than can be handled. For example, a form on a website can be flooded with hundreds or thousands of input terms all at once in the hope of the flood causing the site to crash or become unresponsive.

## Form-Based Authentication

Form-Based Authentication uses forms on a webpage to ask a user to input their username and password.

## Hardening

Hardening is the process of identifying vulnerabilities in a computer system and resolving those vulnerabilities.

## Hash

An algorithm that computes a value based on an object. The has value that is generated is generally much smaller than the object itself.

## Honey pot

A honey pot is a trap set up by the owner of a system to entice others to attempt to gain access to the system.

## HTTP Proxy

An HTTP Proxy is a server that acts as a middleman in communications between a computer or smartphone and a server.

### HTTP (Hypertext Transfer Protocol)

A way (or protocol) of accessing and transporting hypertext documents over the Internet.

### HTTPS

A secure version of HTTP. When a URL is specified with HTTPS: at the beginning, the website and pages are being accessed securely. Banks and other financial institutions typically use HTTPS.

### Hyperlink

A hyperlink is typically a word that is highlighted or underlined on a web page. The link (or URL) is the address on the Internet that the user will be taken too when the hyperlink is clicked.

### Hypertext Markup Language (HTML)

A language used to describe how a web page, and the various elements in the page, is displayed. The web browser interprets the HTML codes in order to display the web page correctly.

### Internet Protocol (IP)

The method (known as a protocol) by which data is sent from one computer to another over the Internet.

### Intrusion Detection

An IDS is a security system for computers and networks that analyzes information to identify possible security breaches. Intrusions are normally attacks that originate from outside the organization.

### IP Address

A way of identifying and addressing a computer on a network. Similar to your physical house address.

### IP Spoofing

A technique of supplying a false IP address. This technique is used by hackers to hide their real address so that hacking activity cannot be traced back to them. In the example of the physical house address above, a spoofed address would, for example, lead the police to a house on the other side of town.

### Malicious Code

A software program that carries a damaging payload. For example, the malicious code might delete all the contacts from your smartphone.

### Malware

A generic term for a number of different types of malicious code. Malware is essentially malicious software which does something unwanted to a computer, smartphone, or tablet.

## Man In The Middle Attack (MITM)

A technique where the hacker 'sits' between two targets and relays messages between them. The targets think they are talking directly to each other, not realizing that they are really talking to the hacker.

## Password Cracking

Password cracking is the process of guessing passwords, given some hints.

## Password Sniffing

A technique of using tools to watch for passwords, usually achieved by analyzing 'traffic' on a network.

## Payload

A payload is the thing that the virus, Trojan, worm or other malicious software develops. A typical payload may be to delete content from the computer or smartphone.

## Penetration

The method of gaining unauthorized access to a computer or network, bypassing the security systems in place.

## Penetration Testing

The method of testing the external perimeter security systems of a network or computer system.

## Phishing

The use of e-mails that appear to originate from a trusted source (such as a bank or reputable company) to trick the user into entering their valid credentials at a fake website. You've probably seen emails like this that say they come from your bank or financial institution.

## Plaintext

Ordinary readable text before it is encrypted into ciphertext, or after it has been decrypted.

## Public Key

The publicly-disclosed part of a pair of cryptographic keys used for asymmetric cryptography.

## Public Key Encryption

A synonym for "asymmetric cryptography".

## Reverse Engineering

Acquiring sensitive data or code by disassembling and analyzing the design of a system component or program. Anti-virus developers frequently have to reverse engineer virus code to determine how it was written and what it is capable of doing.

## Rootkit

A set of programs that a hacker can use to gain access to a computer or computer network.

## Secure Shell (SSH)

A program used to log into another computer over a network. The secure shell allows you to execute commands on the remote machine, and to move files from one machine to another.

## Secure Sockets Layer (SSL)

A method of transmitting private documents over the Internet. SSL was developed by Netscape and works by using a public key to encrypt data that is transferred over the SSL connection.

## Session

A session is a virtual connection between two hosts by which network traffic is passed. Sessions can be kept in 'state' by cookies on your web browser, enabling you to log back onto the site and carry on from where you left off previously.

## Session Hijacking

A method by which a hacker can take over a session that someone else has established.

## Session Key

In the context of symmetric encryption, a key that is temporary or is used for a relatively short period of time. Usually, a session key is used for a defined period of communication between two computers, such as for the duration of a single connection or transaction set, or the key is used in an application that protects relatively large amounts of data and, therefore, needs to be re-keyed frequently.

## Sniffer

A sniffer is a tool that monitors network traffic as it passes through a network interface.

## Sniffing

The process of monitoring network traffic as it passes through a network interface.

## Social Engineering

A method of gaining information or access to computer systems or other entities by using means such as impersonation, tricks, bribes, blackmail, lies and threats.

## Spam

Junk email or junk newsgroup postings.

## Spoof

An attempt to gain access to a system by an unauthorized user posing as an authorized user.

## SQL Injection

A method of gaining access to a database-driven website or application by inserting SQL code into the database, thus manipulating the contents.

## Stealthing

Stealthing is a term used to describe the way that viruses and other forms of malicious code attempts to conceal itself on an infected or compromised system.

## Threat

A potential for a violation of security that can cause harm to a computer system.

## Threat Assessment

A threat assessment is the identification of various types of threats that a computer system, network, or organization might be exposed to.

## Threat Vector

The method that a threat uses to reach its target.

## Trojan Horse

A program that purports to do one thing while doing something completely different. For example, a typical Trojan may appear to be a game, but while in use may be erasing content from the device.

## Virus

A computer program that can replicate, often by attaching its code to other computer programs. Viruses are normally hidden, so under normal conditions are invisible to the user unless they decide to deliver a payload.

## War Driving

War driving is the process of driving around a neighbourhood looking for wireless access point signals that can be used to gain access to unsecured wireless networks.

## Worm

A computer program that runs and can propagate a complete working version of itself onto other hosts on a network, and may consume computer resources destructively. Worms do not replicate by themselves (otherwise they would be viruses).

## Zero-day attack

Day Zero (or Zero Day) is the day a new vulnerability is made known. In some cases, a zero day exploit is referred to as an exploit for which no patch currently available.

###

# Acknowledgements

This eBook would not have been possible without the input, support and assistance of many people.

I won't be able to mention everyone here, so I'll keep it brief. First and foremost, thank you to my beautiful wife, Yvonne. I'm sure you've heard the saying: *"Behind every great man, there's a woman"*. Well, in my case, it's: *"Behind the man, there's a great woman"*. How she puts up with me, I'll never know.

Thank you to my troublesome, but lovable kids Lucas, Llywelyn, Trieve, and Indiana. How I put up with *them*, I'll never know. Thanks to my mum, Veronica for the guidance you've always provided Thanks to Kenny, Gemma, Karl, and all of my family and friends – it's appreciated!

# About the Author

Rod Cambridge is a computer security expert based in London, England. Rod has worked in the computer security industry for the last twenty years in a variety of positions, including technical support, development and technical writing, and has 4 granted US patents in his name in the area of computer security.

Rod has a passion for mobile computing, which started back in the eighties when he worked on a cutting-edge Electronic Point of Sale (EPoS) project based on Psion's handheld Organiser product for Marks and Spencer - a major UK retailer.

After Apple released their first Newton device in 1993, Rod entered a competition run by Apple UK to design an application or service for the fledgling device. While he didn't win, his NewtonPoint proposal came in at a very respectable second place - winning Rod the usage of a Mac for three months, together with all the development software he'd need to produce a proof-of-concept of his proposal.

NewtonPoint was a system that would provide the user with location-specific information beamed via infrared from strategically placed points (NewtonPoints) to their Newton. For example, the NewtonPoint at the entrance to a shopping mall would beam a map of the mall to the user's Newton, together with any special offers, etc. as the user entered the mall.

Due to the fact that the infrastructure required would be much too costly, (and risky), to implement, NewtonPoint didn't proceed any further after Rod completed the proof-of-concept of the client software. That this idea was proposed by Rod in the early nineties, however, shows his credentials as a visionary and forward-thinking individual; Way before GPS in handhelds was proposed, Rod saw the importance of location-specific services for handheld devices.

Jump forward to spring 2006 when Rod announced his innovative website expodition.com. Expodition provided users of Apple's iPod with another location-aware service by allowing them to type in a postcode (zip code) of the area they were travelling to, in order to receive a 'snapshot' of that area in a format that could be viewed on an iPod.

iPods of 2006 vintage were mainly text-based, and so the snapshots provided by Expodition were text files compiled on-the-fly by the PHP scripts running on the back-end of the website. In addition, these snapshots were personalized and tailored to each user based on the user's profile, which specified tastes such as favourite types of food, whether the user liked pubs, clubs, museums, etc.

The service provided by Expodition was groundbreaking - mainly because it gave iPods a new purpose for travelling users. Now, in addition to getting music and video from their iPods, users were also able to get detailed information about their intended destination.

Unfortunately for Rod, six months after Expodition went live, Apple announced the iPhone; with it's advanced OS and built-in support for location-awareness. This leap in technology had an adverse effect on the service provided by Expodition, witnessed by a steady decline in usage of the site after the iPhone shipped. In addition, when the iPod touch was introduced a few months later, it became obvious that Expodition would not be the success that Rod had hoped.

In 2009, Rod launched his first iPhone app, Top-Tens, which allows users to keep track of a number of top 10 lists, such as the top 10 books on Amazon.com or songs on iTunes. In total, almost 100 different top 10 lists can be tracked by the app.

Rod continues to innovate, and in 2011 released his first eBook. Rod has many more of these planned.

**Contacting the Author**

Rod would love to hear from you. Probably the easiest way to get in touch is via his website: www.HowNotToBooks.co.uk. Any updates, downloads or errata that might be available for this eBook will be posted there.

Any feedback received, both positive and negative, will be welcome. In addition, Rod will also do his best to reply to each comment as it's received although, due to volume, this may not always be possible.

You can email Rod directly at: rod@hownottobooks.co.uk or follow him on Twitter @appdebut.

iPod, iPhone, iPad and their associated trademarks are copyright Apple Computer. Other trademarks mentioned in this eBook are copyright their respective owners.

www.ingramcontent.com/pod-product-compliance
Lightning Source LLC
Chambersburg PA
CBHW061C18050326
40689CE00012B/2672